The Loch Ness Monster

New and future titles in the series include:

The Mystery Library

The Loch Ness Monster

Thomas Streissguth

LUCENT BOOKS
SAN DIEGO, CALIFORNIA

THOMSON

GALE

Detroit • New York • San Diego • San Francisco
Boston • New Haven, Conn. • Waterville, Maine
London • Munich

Library of Congress Cataloging-in-Publication Data

Streissguth, Thomas, 1958–
    The Loch Ness Monster / by Thomas Streissguth.
      p. cm. — (The mystery library)
Includes bibliographical references and index.
Summary: Discusses the possible existence of the Loch Ness
monster including alleged sightings and photographs, investigations
and research conducted at Loch Ness, and the possible origins of and
explanations for the monster.
    ISBN 1-56006-772-1 (alk. paper)
    1. Loch Ness monster—Juvenile literature. [1. Loch Ness
monster. 2. Monsters.] I. Title. II. Mystery Library (Lucent
Books).
    QL89.2.L6 S94 2002
    001.944—dc21

2001006131

Contents

Foreword

In Shakespeare's immortal play *Hamlet*, the young Danish aristocrat Horatio has clearly been astonished and disconcerted by his encounter with a ghostlike apparition on the castle battlements. "There are more things in heaven and earth," his friend Hamlet assures him, "than are dreamt of in your philosophy."

Many people today would readily agree with Hamlet that the world and the vast universe surrounding it are teeming with wonders and oddities that remain largely outside the realm of present human knowledge or understanding. How did the universe begin? What caused the dinosaurs to become extinct? Was the lost continent of Atlantis a real place or merely legendary? Does a monstrous creature lurk beneath the surface of Scotland's Loch Ness? These are only a few of the intriguing questions that remain unanswered, despite the many great strides made by science in recent centuries.

Lucent Books' Mystery Library series is dedicated to exploring these and other perplexing, sometimes bizarre, and often disturbing or frightening wonders. Each volume in the series presents the best-known tales, incidents, and evidence surrounding the topic in question. Also included are the opinions and theories of scientists and other experts who have attempted to unravel and solve the ongoing mystery. And supplementing this information is a fulsome list of sources for further reading, providing the reader with the means to pursue the topic further.

The Mystery Library will satisfy every young reader's fascination for the unexplained. As one of history's greatest scientists, physicist Albert Einstein, put it:

The most beautiful thing we can experience is the mysterious. It is the source of all true art and science. He to whom this emotion is a stranger, who can no longer wonder and stand rapt in awe, is as good as dead: his eyes are closed.

A Mysterious Monster

April 14, 1933, began as an ordinary day for John Mackay and his wife. They were driving along the A82, a paved roadway that had just been completed on the north shore of Loch Ness, a long and narrow lake set among the steep bluffs and hillsides of the Scottish Highlands. The chilly spring weather would soon give way to a milder summer, when daylight would last past midnight and the heather and gorse would paint these hillsides in vivid purple, yellow, and green.

The Mackays could not have been prepared for what they saw that day in the lake: A long, dark creature resembling a huge snake slowly rose from the surface and then vanished. It was too big to be a seal or an otter; it could not have been a boat; it moved in a way that no tree trunk, rock, or mat of vegetation could move.

The Mackays told Alexander Campbell, a local "water bailiff," about their sighting. It was Campbell's job to patrol the waters of Loch Ness and attend to any crimes or accidents on the lake. Campbell described the incident to a reporter for the *Inverness Courier*, the local newspaper. The story soon spread to the rest of Britain and to sensation-hungry reporters in London.

The Mackays were the first people to see the Loch Ness "monster" since the building of the A82 highway in the summer of 1932. To build the highway, construction crews had blasted out the road grade from the steep hillsides. They had also cut the heavy screen of trees that had blocked the view of the lake from the old road on the north side. Some locals speculated that the construction had brought about the sighting. The noise, dust, and vibration of the work may have disturbed wildlife in and around the lake; plus, the new views over the lake made its surface and shores easily visible.

In the coming years, many more sightings would occur. A number of people who lived along Loch Ness came forward with their own strange tales of a huge fish, or lizard, or dragon, or something else that swam in the loch, popping above the surface for a few seconds to startle observers. Most people who reported such sightings knew of many more that

A woman gazes out over Urquhart Castle and Loch Ness in 1930.

had been kept under wraps for a long time by witnesses who feared public ridicule and the skepticism of experts. Soon, crowds of tourists appeared along the A82, their eyes peeled and their cameras ready. Hunting for the Loch Ness monster became a favorite pastime in the Highlands.

The Loch Ness monster remained half legend and half joke for most people until the 1960s, when scientists began taking the legend more seriously. By that time, industrious reporters had collected hundreds of eyewitness sightings from reliable sources (as well as some obvious jokes and hoaxes). The Loch Ness monster, it seemed, did not match the description of any known fish, reptile, or amphibian. To prove the monster's existence, scientists brought still cameras, sonar, film, and organization to the great hunt. Teams of observers combed the surface with cameras and plumbed the depths with sonar in an attempt to search every corner of a deep, cold, and very cloudy lake. Famous national museums and institutions sponsored the hunts, which were led by naturalists renowned for their knowledge and experience.

Despite these efforts, the Loch Ness monster would not appear. There were curious anomalies on film and on the sonar record, but none that would put the monster's existence beyond any doubt. By the 1990s, the expeditions had ended, the equipment was dismantled, and the lake was again left in relative peace and quiet. The sightings continued, but no monster was captured and proven to exist. Today, Loch Ness still attracts visitors in search of natural beauty and a firsthand look at an old and curious puzzle. But the lake still keeps its secrets.

Chapter 1

The Legend

For centuries, people have told tales of strange and terrifying beasts rising from the waters. During the Age of Exploration, when Europeans set out for the distant regions of the seven seas, massive sea serpents were blamed for unexplained disappearances of many ships. Sea serpents were spotted in the South Atlantic, in Massachusetts Bay, and off the coast of California.

Just as the seas had their serpents and monsters—real and imaginary—so did smaller rivers and lakes. For the people of Scotland, the northernmost part of the British Isles, there were a few long and very deep lakes where it was easy for the imagination to run wild. One such lake, known as Loch Ness, seemed a fitting place for fantastic legends. The largest and deepest body of freshwater in the British Isles, Loch Ness lies in the Great Glen, a valley that divides northern Scotland along a geologic fault line. The floor of the valley is made up of breccia, loose and fragmented rock that was ground down by glacial ice during the last ice age, which ended about ten thousand years ago. Since that time, the glen has filled with freshwater and is now a series of narrow valleys and lakes.

Loch Ness runs twenty-three miles from its southwestern shore, at Fort William, to the northeast, where it meets the Caledonian Canal and the River Ness, which empties into the North Sea at the city of Inverness. The lake averages only a mile wide, but the bottom of the lake lies, in places, more than seven hundred feet below the surface. There are few beaches or shallows—the lake bottom runs nearly straight down from the shore (at one point, it reaches a depth of five

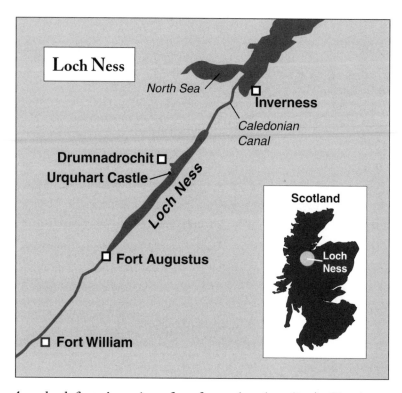

hundred feet, just sixty feet from the shoreline). Six rivers drain into the lake, which holds more than two cubic miles of water, making it the third largest lake by volume in all of Europe. There is little to see even close to the surface, however, because the murky lake is filled with decayed vegetation, known as peat, that washes down from the hillsides.

Because it lies along a fault line, Loch Ness is occasionally plagued by earthquakes. In 1755, a few weeks after a massive earthquake destroyed the city of Lisbon, a thousand miles to the south, Loch Ness was rocked by an earth tremor. For several hours, the waters of the lake sloshed back and forth, rising several feet above normal at the north and south ends. A moderate earthquake struck the Great Glen in 1816, and smaller tremors hit in 1888, 1890, and 1901.

The lake could be a very dangerous place for those who ventured out from shore. Many swimmers had disappeared in the freezing water, their bodies never to be found. Many small watercraft had also disappeared in the sudden storms that swept along the valley, where the wind and the weather could turn in a minute. Those who traveled on the lake always took care to get home before night fell.

The Picts, St. Columba, and the Monster

For centuries, the people of Loch Ness have also seen something more unusual, and more frightening, than bad weather. The Picts, the ancient inhabitants of the Highlands region, recorded what appears to be a lake monster in the chiseled surface of massive standing stones. Stephen Lyons, author of a PBS television show on the Loch Ness monster, describes the Pictish beast:

> From the carved, standing stones still found in the region around Loch Ness, it is clear the Picts were fascinated by animals, and careful to render them

Loch Ness is the largest and deepest body of freshwater in the British Isles.

with great fidelity. All the animals depicted on the Pictish stones are lifelike and easily recognizable—all but one. The exception is a strange beast with an elongated beak or muzzle, a head locket or spout, and flippers instead of feet. Described by some scholars as a swimming elephant, the Pictish beast is the earliest known evidence for an idea that has held sway in the Scottish Highlands for at least 1,500 years—that Loch Ness is home to a mysterious aquatic animal.[1]

The written lore of the Loch Ness monster dates back to the seventh century A.D. and the Abbot of Iona's "Life of St. Columba." Writing to glorify the deeds of the saint who had converted the Picts to Christianity, the abbot described how the saint once saved a man from a monster dwelling in the icy waters of the River Ness:

St. Columba raises his hand and speaks to the monster—driving it away.

The monster . . . was lying at the bottom of the stream, and when it felt the water disturbed above by the man swimming, [it] suddenly rushed out, and, giving an awful roar, darted after him, with its mouth wide open, as the man swam in the middle of the stream. Then the blessed man [St. Columba] observing this, raised his holy hand, while all the rest, brethren as well as strangers, were stupefied with terror, and, invoking the name of God, formed the saving sign of the cross in the air, and commanded the ferocious monster, saying, "Thou shalt go no further, nor touch the man; go back with all speed." Then at the voice of the saint, the monster was terrified, and fled more quickly than if it had been pulled back with ropes, though it had just got so near to Lugne, as he swam, that there was not more than the length of a spear-staff between the man and the beast. Then the brethren seeing that the monster had gone back, and that their comrade Lugne returned to them in the boat safe and sound, were struck with admiration, and gave glory to God in the blessed man. And even the barbarous heathens, who were present, were forced by the greatness of this miracle, which they themselves had seen, to magnify the God of the Christians.[2]

For this story, the Abbot of Iona may have relied on certain legends that were common in the Highlands. It was said that people who drowned in Loch Ness and other deep lakes were the victims of kelpies, or water horses that lived beneath the surface. With their cheerful neighing, these creatures lured men to climb onto their backs, then galloped into the nearest lake or river, drowning their trusting riders. Adding to these legends was the fact that the bodies of the drowned very rarely reappeared on the surface of the lakes or along their shores.

In his book *The Loch Ness Monster: The Evidence*, Steuart Campbell explains the origins of these lake monster myths:

In Ireland, where the Scots originated, the country people supposed that this world [i.e., the world on land] is duplicated underwater, and they told tales of cows, bulls, dogs, and horses from that other-world. . . . If water was the domain of the other-world, then those who ventured onto lakes were violating that world and were in danger of punishment. Necessarily folklore must have developed around this concept, and any unusual lake phenomenon must have been interpreted as a manifestation of this underworld.[3]

Nahuelito, the Monster of Patagonia

The remote and ruggedly beautiful region of Patagonia covers southern Argentina. Here, as in the Highlands of Scotland, the local people have long heard tales of a lake monster, Nahuelito, of Nahuel Huapi Lake. Dozens of tourists and residents who live along the lake have seen a snakelike creature, from 15 to 150 feet long, cross the surface of the lake. The sightings usually take place in summer, when the wind is calm and the lake's waters are still.

The modern age of the Nahuelito began in 1922, when the newspapers in Argentina reported the sighting of the monster by an American named Martin Sheffield. Scientists and zoologists speculated that Sheffield had seen a plesiosaur, a survivor from the age of the dinosaurs. Others weren't so sure.

Twelve years before, Nahuelito had been seen by George Garrett, an Englishman who ran a local business. As quoted in Mark Chorvinsky's Internet article "Nahuelito, Patagonian Lake Monster," Garrett later testified to the *Toronto Globe* that:

We were beating windward up an inlet called Pass Coytrue, which bounded the peninsula. This inlet was about five miles in length, a mile or so in width, and of an unfathomable depth. Just as we were near the rocky shore of the peninsula, before tacking, I happened to look astern towards the center of the inlet, and, to my great surprise, I saw about a quarter of a mile to leeward, an object which appeared to be 15 or 20 feet in diameter, and perhaps six feet above the water. . . . On mentioning my experience to my neighbours, they said the Indians often spoke of immense water animals they had seen from time to time.

Some believe that Nahuelito and Nessie, of Scotland's Loch Ness, are one and the same, and that the Loch Ness monster swims the eight thousand miles to Argentina each year, either for the winter warmth of the southern hemisphere or just for a vacation.

The kelpie was one of the many legendary monsters of medieval times. Griffins, sphinxes, dragons, and other strange and terrifying hybrids inhabited remote places—mountaintops, caves, dark forest glens, and deep lakes. To the Celtic inhabitants of Ireland and Scotland, lakes and rivers were portals into the other world, an invisible realm where fertile imaginations overcame the evidence of the senses.

The Monster Reappears

During the Middle Ages, few writers took the time to set down such legends in a permanent record. Monster stories were regarded as mere folklore, common knowledge that was not worthy of the valuable parchment used for describing and remembering things. Every lake and river in Scotland held some kind of water spirit, and one did best simply to stay away from the water. The people of medieval Scotland had more pressing problems to deal with: civil war, famine, plague, and the raids of marauding Vikings, who believed in lake monsters themselves and who carved the images of such beasts into the prows of their ships. As Henry H. Bauer wrote in *The Enigma of Loch Ness,* "The Viking ship, with its high prow shaped like a long neck and dragon-like head, was deliberately designed to

The Vikings believed in lake monsters and carved images of them into the prows of their ships.

look like a water monster and to strike fear into the onlooker; the approach of these 'sea serpents' in fact boded ill for settlements marked by the Vikings as their prey."[4]

In the eighteenth century, also known in Europe as the Age of Enlightenment, writers and historians dismissed lake monsters and other legends as nothing more than local superstitions. As scientists and philosophers developed a more practical knowledge of the natural world, such superstitions were expected to slowly disappear into the history books.

But the stories and superstitions would not disappear. Loch Lomond—the largest lake in Scotland in terms of surface area—had its "beasties," as did Loch Tay and Loch Rannoch. The deepest lake in Scotland, Loch Morar, had dozens of sightings and legends of its own. In 1850, a landowner who had a small loch on his property, Loch Beiste, tried to trap a monster by completely draining his lake, then setting out quicklime in order to poison it. He failed to capture anything.

From time to time, strange things also happened at Loch Ness. Sometimes these occurrences could not be explained; at other times, they could. In 1852, the *Inverness Courier* reported that two large animals were seen swimming in Loch Ness. Many farmers and other local residents quickly armed themselves with pitchforks and rifles to drive the intruders away. Soon, however, it was revealed that the monsters were nothing more than a pair of ponies on the loose from a pasture near the lake.

In Europe and in North America, some individuals took advantage of people's interest in sea serpents and other legendary creatures. One of the best lake-monster hoaxes was carried out in Wyoming County, New York, and is described by Steuart Campbell in *The Loch Ness Monster: The Evidence*:

On the evening of 13 July 1855 a group of "honest, temperate, and industrious" men and boys, who were out fishing, sighted an 18m long creature which, they

The Giant Squid Appears

Tales and sightings of sea monsters were so common in the nineteenth century that nearly everybody had a theory on what the creatures really were. Some conjectured that sea monsters were actually giant squids, ugly beasts with eight long tentacles, a pair of malevolent eyes, and a taste for fishing boats. Many sailors reported seeing such a squid, but respectable scientists dismissed it as yet another figment of the fertile human imagination.

Then, on October 26, 1873, in Conception Bay, Newfoundland, two herring fishermen began poking at a purplish mass lying on the surface. Suddenly, tentacles rose from the sea, gathering the boat toward a gaping open mouth. One of the fishermen desperately hacked at the arms with a hatchet, finally driving it off. All that was left was a strange, inky fluid where a very real giant squid had attacked—and a long section of tentacle that remained behind in the boat and was brought ashore to prove the unbelievable tale.

A huge squid attacks a galleon.

alleged, chased them to shore. They described it as a serpent 18–30m long, shiny, dark green with yellow spots, flaming red eyes, a mouth and huge fins. Thousands visited the village of Perry and expeditions were mounted. Two years later, as the result of a fire, the hoax was discovered. Two people confessed that they had built the monster out of waterproof canvas, paint and wire, and that it was towed by ropes and made to surface by pumping in air.[5]

The First Hoax

In 1868, the first monster hoax at Loch Ness occurred. A party of fishermen captured a dolphin, skinned it, and then left it ashore at the village of Abriachan for local people to discover. For several days, the news spread that a strange, monstrously large amphibian had washed ashore. Then the practical joke was exposed. Unusual creatures did appear naturally from time to time, however. In 1871, a seven-foot-long sturgeon, a fish that is not native to Loch Ness, was caught in the River Ness, the waterway that passes through Inverness and empties into the North Sea.

Loch Ness was not the only place in Scotland where strange creatures were appearing. Loch Hourn was the sight of another strange event, seen by credible witnesses, in August 1872. Reverends John Macrae and David Twopeny, along with Gilbert Bogle and three children, set out for a day of fishing. The party descended to the Sound of Sleat, between the Scottish mainland and the Island of Skye. Soon after getting under way, the group saw a dark form rise behind their cutter. The creature seemed to have several humps and to be about sixty feet long. It followed them for several hours, until it became too dark to see. After resting for the night on shore, the party resumed their journey the next day—only to spot the persistent creature again. Macrae and Twopeny described the monster as having a long neck, a head like a horse, and several humps in its back.

At Loch Ness, more sightings were reported in the 1880s. A mason named Alexander MacDonald, who commuted on Loch Ness every day by steamer, claimed he often saw the monster swimming about in the loch. Roderick Matheson, who owned a sailboat and often traveled on Loch

Ness, once saw a giant eel with a neck and mane that made it look, to him, like an aquatic horse. A young boy named H.J. Craig was fishing with his brother in 1889 when an unidentifiable animal, resembling a huge serpent, suddenly sprang out of the water.

In December 1903, a man named Frazer and two companions saw what they believed to be an upturned boat floating not far from them. But when they rowed over to have a look, the thing swam away. Another incident occurred during World War I, as author Peter Costello explains:

> One evening the head keeper at Balmacaan Estate, James Cameron, came into the bar of the Drumnadrochit Hotel and asked for a large brandy. Later he told [Kenneth] Mackay, who had insisted on walking part of the way home with him, what had so affected him. While he had been out fishing on the

Strange creatures like this sturgeon have been reported in Loch Ness.

loch an "enormous animal" had surfaced beside his boat. The shock made him dizzy and he fell to the bottom of the boat. He would not say more and swore Mackay to secrecy.[6]

A local resident named Winifred Cary recalled her first sighting of the Loch Ness monster in 1917:

> When I was 11 years old, my brother and I were out in a boat, fishing, trolling for salmon, you see. As we were going east along the pier, there suddenly rose up in the middle of the loch not near the boat, fortunately, this colossal thing like a great whale. It was going fast against the wind and was only up for a second or two. Of course, no one believed us when we told them.[7]

Local residents search Loch Ness for signs of a monster in 1933.

Many more sightings of the Loch Ness monster followed. Boaters, fishermen, and tourists reported seeing disturbances

in the water, smooth objects rising from the surface, and rounded humps moving rapidly across the lake. Many saw lizardlike bodies, long necks, and heads poking through the waves. A few people saw large black creatures moving along or across the nearby roads at night.

The Mackay sighting of April 1933 set off a monster mania in Great Britain. Newspaper articles about Loch Ness appeared almost daily, and monster-hunting tourists arrived at the lake in hopes of catching a glimpse of "Nessie," as the monster was nicknamed. As Bernard Heuvelmans writes in *In the Wake of the Sea Serpents*,

> After the first encouraging reports, the atmosphere was soon vitiated by blatant hoaxes, gibes at the expense of the Highlanders' fondness for whisky and gift for second sight. There was a flood of journalism, much of it sensational or ill-informed, and peremptory statements by so-called experts. In this glare of dubious publicity genuine research was almost impossible.[8]

On July 22, 1933, the Loch Ness monster was seen on land by a Mr. and Mrs. Spicer. Once again, the sighting took place in the late afternoon, around 4:00 P.M. Mr. Spicer described what happened in a letter to the *Inverness Courier*:

> I saw the nearest approach to a dragon or pre-historic animal that I have ever seen in my life. . . . It seemed to have a long neck which moved up and down in the manner of a scenic railway, and the body was fairly big, with a high back; but if there were any feet they must have been of the web kind, and as for a tail I cannot say, as it moved so rapidly, and when we got to the spot it had probably disappeared into the loch. . . .
>
> Whatever it is, and it may be a land and water animal, I think it should be destroyed, as I am not sure whether I had been quite so close to it I should have cared to tackle it.[9]

What had the Spicers seen? The newspaper itself claimed that the creature may have been an otter. At that time of day, an otter scurrying across the road, perhaps carrying one of its young in its mouth, might trick the fallible human eye into believing it had seen something quite different.

Footprints

That summer, the *London Daily Mail* hired a professional film director and big-game hunter, Marmaduke A. Wetherall, to flush the Loch Ness monster from its lair. In a blare of publicity, Wetherall arrived at the lakeshore with binoculars and a box camera. A few days later, evidence appeared: Fresh, deep footprints of some large, four-toed animal were pressed into the soft soil along the shore where they stood. Wetherall predicted that the unknown animal was about twenty feet long. He took plaster casts of the footprints and sent them to the Natural History Museum in London.

The prints and the casts were closely examined, and the museum scientists soon identified where the footprints had come from. Wetherall had discovered the hoofs of an elephant. Shortly after, the truth was revealed. After hearing of the Wetherall expedition, a resident of Loch Ness and his two sons had stolen down to the waterside one night and pressed their elephant-hoof umbrella stand into the earth.

Hoax or no hoax, the eyewitness sightings continued. In 1935, Rena MacKenzie saw a long neck and a small head emerge from the water for a full five minutes. Two years later, William Mackay and a group of cricket players saw two gray humps, about three feet high, in the water. Mackay saw exactly the same thing a few years later while looking at the lake through a telescope. Since first hearing from John Mackay and writing his piece for the *Inverness Courier*, water bailiff Alex Campbell claimed to see the Loch Ness monster again and again. He described it as about thirty feet in length, with a head and neck about five feet long, and having a shy nature: The monster always dipped out of sight when a boat approached it.

In the meantime, Loch Ness and the Highlands were attracting hordes of tourists, curiosity seekers, and believers. On certain weekends, a long parade of cars could be spotted snaking along the hillsides with passengers searching and cameras poised and necks craned for a glimpse of the beast. Hotels were filled in the summers. The city of Inverness spent little money to promote itself, for the Loch Ness sightings had brought as much publicity as it needed. Searching for and sighting the monster became a sort of national pastime in Great Britain, and many people returned home from the lake with a good story to tell about something strange they had spotted in the water.

Chapter 2

Early Investigations

At one time, the sightings of lake monsters and sea serpents might have aroused fear and wonder in those who heard of them. But the early twentieth century was a poor time to be spinning incredible tales of improbable happenings. The natural world was under close examination by biologists, zoologists, geologists, and the new breed of paleontologists who specialized in the remains of extinct species. These specialists employed a new way of looking at the world, in which theories had to be proven by physical evidence and experiments had to be repeated several times before their conclusions could be accepted. To this new breed, ancient legends and eyewitness reports, no matter who was relating them, proved nothing at all.

Those who did not call themselves "scientists," and who did not have expertise in scientific fields, were still beginning to accept the scientific method and believe that nothing was real until proven by science. In many ways, scientific theories were making their lives longer and more comfortable. The myths and old wives' tales that had once guided day-to-day life began to retreat into history books, where they could be studied solely for one's curiosity and entertainment. In the meantime, most people believed that science would take over the investigation of the Loch Ness monster and solve this mystery once and for all.

Eyewitness sightings at Loch Ness were fine for newspapers and popular magazines, but they did not provide enough evidence for scientists, who preferred well-tested theories over well-told tales. The ordinary person out for a stroll or a drive along the lake could conjure up anything out of the imagination, or simply spread a tall tale to win some attention. Scientists need something they can look at, examine, and analyze. Before they could believe in the Loch Ness monster, someone would have to find it, capture it, and drag it ashore. As Loch Ness author Henry H. Bauer explains,

The claimed discovery of the so-called Loch Ness monster in the 1930s was for biologists a statement in a void; it did not point to anything they could usefully do. The available information was insufficient to identify the animal, there were no specimens whose morphology [structure] or behavior could be studied, and no one could tell how to get such information.

Paleontologists examine the remains of a mammoth. Many people believe advancing science like paleontology will help solve the mystery of the Loch Ness monster.

And that still applies: reported sightings are far too infrequent, brief, and uninformative to make it reasonable for a scientist to spend at Loch Ness the time needed for the activities of his career.[10]

Acceptable Evidence

Acceptable scientific evidence begins with photographs. In the 1930s, the first still photographs of the monster were taken and developed. Since that time, tourists, searchers, and scientists have taken hundreds of above-water photographs of unidentified objects. There have been films and sonar readings as well. Much of this evidence has a legend of its own—of tampering, trickery, and elaborate hoaxes meant to impress the gullible. Yet many of the Loch Ness photos are genuine. And the objects they show fit the scientific description of a plesiosaur, a creature with a long neck, flipperlike limbs, a humped back, and a massive trunk.

On April 19, 1934, a doctor from London, Robert Kenneth Wilson, took the first photograph of what was said to be the Loch Ness monster. The picture showed a long neck and a small head—the spitting image of an ancient dinosaur, as many people imagined the monster to be. The *London Daily Mail* carried the picture on April 21, and Wilson gained a permanent place in the history of the Loch Ness mystery. Finally, there was photographic proof, and many believed that even more solid evidence, such as a living or dead specimen, would soon follow.

The people living near Loch Ness had little trouble believing in Wilson's picture or in the eyewitness reports. As Richard Frere, who grew up near the lake, remembers,

In those days before the war on our regular visits to the Loch we several times saw powerful washes, lines of humps and once a thin, attenuated neck passing like a great swan's behind winter trees which stood between road and water. Late one evening, after a moonlight descent from the crags above Abriachan, we heard a mighty splash in the Loch and scrambled down to the shore in time to see a ring of glittering waves emanating from a central turbulence. Not one of us doubted the origin of these phenomena; it would have been almost heretical to do so. We had every faith in our plesiosaur and although everybody wanted a good photograph it would only have brought final proof of something which we already knew to be true.[11]

The "surgeon's photograph" and the eyewitness sightings of 1933 and 1934 prompted the first organized investigation of Loch Ness. Sir Edward Mountain, a wealthy business executive, hired twenty unemployed workers from Inverness and placed them in strategic lookouts around the lake. He paid the workers two British pounds a week to keep an eye out all day long, every day, for five weeks. Eleven sightings were reported and five photographs taken, but none of them showed anything that looked clearly like a lake monster.

Robert Kenneth Wilson's famous photograph of the Loch Ness monster.

These two photographs, taken during Sir Edward Mountain's investigation in 1934, supposedly capture two sightings of the Loch Ness monster.

Regardless of the quality, photographs occasionally appeared alongside the many Loch Ness articles, lending at least a shadowy appearance of proof. Over time, these pictures have been very scrupulously catalogued and considered by Loch Ness monster experts. Some are too grainy to prove anything, and others have been revealed as out-and-out hoaxes. But there are a few well-known Loch Ness photographs, and evidence recorded in other media such as film and sonar, that cannot be so easily dismissed.

The Loch Ness Monster: The Movie

Still photographs capture an instant in time and show things that can easily delude the eye. When a scientist examines the Loch Ness photographs, he or she might not see a monster but, rather, a dark, unidentifiable shape surrounded by water. It could be a log, the tail of an otter, or an overturned boat.

Movie film and videotape provide more concrete evidence. Exposing several seconds of film to the erratic motions of a mysterious shape in the water seemed to make the Loch Ness monster more real. In the late summer of 1934, the hopeful James Fraser, who had been hired by Sir Mountain for his still-picture project, remained behind at the loch after the end of the project. On September 22, Fraser shot an unidentified swimming object at a distance of about three-quarters of a mile with a 16-millimeter camera (unfortunately, the film was eventually lost). Early one morning in 1935, a Dr. McRae filmed something with a long neck, a long tail, three humps, and small horns splashing and swimming in the water. Unfortunately for researchers, this evidence remains as secretive and elusive as the monster itself. The film is allegedly locked in a London bank vault with instructions that it cannot be released "until such time as the public takes such matters serious!"[12] Since all the trustees are now dead, it is not known who owns the film, and lawyers have been unable to get the film released.

The first color film was taken by G.E. Taylor in May 1938. According to experts who saw it, the "monster" was a mat of vegetation, or perhaps a dead horse floating in the water. While on vacation that summer, a bank manager named James Currie shot a short film of three humps, a long neck, and a small head swimming about three hundred feet from shore. Currie's film, like Dr. McRae's, is said to lie in a bank vault, sealed and unavailable for viewing.

More Investigation

Meanwhile, everyone waited for the day that the monster would poke its head above water for a clear and indisputable photograph or reel of film. A circus offered twenty thousand pounds for its capture, and betting operations in London began setting down the odds for proof that the Loch Ness monster was real. To this day, one can place the same bet.

Eventually, the fever died down. In the 1940s, while Britain was fighting a war and defending its territory against German bombs and a possible invasion, people forgot the Loch Ness sightings and turned their attention to survival. There was no time for tourism and little interest in lake monsters, real or imaginary.

After World War II, Loch Ness monster sightings again claimed space in local newspapers. By this time, however, the

The Science Fiction Age

The early 1960s were prime time for unidentified objects, in the water as well as in the air. The age of extraterrestrial exploration had begun, and rockets were hurtling from the United States and the Soviet Union into the unknown reaches of outer space. Writers speculated on the alien life-forms that might be found, and aluminum rocket models appeared in popular science fiction movies, blasting off from the surface of papier-mâché moons. The mass media began to consider the possibility that alien life-forms were visiting Earth. These aliens might be examining the human race, preparing to defeat it in battle, enslave it, clone it, experiment on it, or simply consume it for dinner.

In a darkened theater, films aim for the suspension of belief—the audience's acceptance that they are seeing real people instead of actors and real places rather than movie sets. Couldn't the same kind of film be exposed to provide support for a mythical beast, to achieve a similar suspension of belief? The short, grainy, and indistinct film shot by Tim Dinsdale in 1960 seemed to provide a very modern form of evidence for the existence of the Loch Ness monster.

people around Loch Ness were getting used to their monster. When they sighted it, they generally kept the news to themselves. Some came forward when asked by researchers from out of town. Others did not want to talk about it.

The Dinsdale Film

For more than twenty years, there had been no more Loch Ness monster movies. Then, in April 1960, an important breakthrough occurred in the Loch Ness investigation. Tim Dinsdale, one of the best-known and most dedicated searchers for the Loch Ness monster, set up a 16-millimeter camera at the window of his car. After five days of no luck, he finally spotted a large oval shape about two-thirds of the way across the lake that suddenly began to move, creating ripples and a wake. The object turned and zigged and zagged as if it were some living being (or perhaps a boat) and not an inanimate object such as a large mat of floating vegetation. Dinsdale turned the movie camera on the object and exposed most of the reel, stopping when he realized he would soon run out of film.

Dinsdale wanted to prove that what he had seen and filmed was not a zigzagging boat. He asked the owner of a nearby hotel, Hugh Rowand, to take a boat out and follow, as best he could, the course that the unknown object had taken. This second film would be compared with the first to determine if the appearance of the boat and the wake following it were different from the appearances on the first film.

The films were developed and very closely examined. The first one definitely showed something moving in the water, but there seemed no way to positively identify it. The *London Daily Mail* printed stills taken from the film, and the British Broadcasting Corporation ran the film on the television program *Panorama*, which aired on June 13, 1960. A new wave of monster mania resulted. Many of those who saw

Tim Dinsdale devoted many years to the search for the Loch Ness monster.

the Dinsdale film were convinced that the Loch Ness monster, whatever it might be, had finally been documented. Others, such as Richard Frere, anxiously awaiting proof of something they had long believed in, felt only disappointment:

> Here was the evidence for which I had confidently waited since, as a boy of eleven, I had first set eyes upon the Loch. But when I saw it at a private viewing later I could not repress a sense of keen disappointment. I was doing a lot of messing about in small boats then, living with them you might even say, and here was simply another one of them. This was no monster but a ten- or twelve-foot wooden dinghy with a small outboard motor. I had seen the same thing too recently and too often, from every angle and every distance, to be mistaken.[13]

Steuart Campbell, in his skeptical book *The Loch Ness Monster: The Evidence*, maintains that Dinsdale had captured nothing more mysterious than a small dinghy moving under the power of a single outboard motor:

> Relevant to interpretation [of the Dinsdale film] is the fact that only two months later, [Loch Ness author Maurice] Burton and his party observed powered dinghies traveling almost the same route as Dinsdale's [object], they even saw them appear to vanish just as Dinsdale had done. Later Burton discovered that a local farmer was in the habit of taking a dinghy across at the very time when Dinsdale was filming.[14]

The famous Dinsdale film was examined closely again in the 1980s. When the contrast of the film was enhanced, the examiners could clearly make out a man sitting in the back of a small boat. Since the color of the boat almost exactly matched the color of the wake it created, it was invisible to Dinsdale on the distant shore. Thus, the best-known film of

Tim Dinsdale Explains Himself

Tim Dinsdale, who died in 1987, was one of the most determined and dedicated Loch Ness researchers. He spent nearly thirty years of his life at Loch Ness, filming, watching, and photographing.

Why did he do it? He once gave the following explanation:

> The cost has been great, at a private level seemingly impossible to meet in time and money, and yet, in meeting it, by some strange alchemy I am the richer for it, and my family no less independent. . . . The Monster justifies itself in terms of opposites; because I do not believe it is in itself important. Dramatic, extraordinary, exciting, a zoological wonder perhaps but not important, in the sense that it's only an animal like an elephant, or for that matter a cow which is equally marvelous.
>
> But in the way it relates to our scientific society, it is of enormous importance. In the case of embarrassing unexplained phenomenon, science just doesn't want to know . . . and for this reason it is imperative that voluntary work continues at

Loch Ness. We stand on new frontiers of discovery which will test the credulence and courage of man, and his ability to adapt. . . . We must have this type of mental outlook, and at Loch Ness we have such a rare opportunity to demonstrate the need for it.

Tim Dinsdale claimed to have caught the Loch Ness monster on film.

the Loch Ness monster turned out to be nothing more than a local resident out for an afternoon ride on the lake.

When the Dinsdale film first surfaced, however, many people were intrigued, and they became determined to solve this mystery once and for all. In 1961, a group of dedicated investigators set up the Loch Ness Investigation Bureau (LNIB) under the leadership of David James, a member of the British Parliament. The LNIB was to be a completely unbiased effort to establish the truth of the Loch Ness monster. James enlisted the help of Constance Whyte, an author who had made the most thorough analysis of the evidence to date in her book *More than a Legend*.

The first research conducted by the Loch Ness Investigation Bureau took place at night, using spotlights to illuminate the lake from the grounds of the Clansman Hotel. Later they set up a telescope watching post near Urquhart Castle and outfitted vans with photographic and film equipment to drive along the lake and keep a sharp lookout. In 1962, volunteers with binoculars and cameras scanned Loch Ness from its shore for telltale signs and disturbances. In the years to come, the search became even more elaborate; a constant watch was kept on the lake day and night in the spring, summer, and early fall. The LNIB used cameras, sonar, helicopters, salmon bait, music piped underwater, and recorded sounds of the sea. James had charges set off to imitate the road blasting of the 1930s, which many speculated had brought the monster to the surface. He had military experts examine photographs and film and brought all evidence to the attention of respected scientists.

An American biochemist named Roy Mackal joined the LNIB expeditions in 1965, bringing more scientific respectability to the hunt. Mackal used every kind of sophisticated photo and radar equipment available, as well as sound recording equipment and specially designed harpoons to take tissue samples. Mackal finally got his own glimpse of the

Loch Ness monster in 1970, when a triangular fin appeared above the water not far from his boat and then slipped beneath the surface. That summer, he described his experience to a group at the Massachusetts Institute of Technology. In the audience that day, Robert Rines, who would devote much of the rest of his life to the hunt for the Loch Ness monster, was listening with rapt attention.

Researchers with the Loch Ness Investigation Bureau watch the lake for signs of the monster in 1968.

Chapter 3

Healthy Skepticism

I n the 1960s, the first full-scale, systematic investigations of Loch Ness took place. Determined once and for all to either find the monster or prove that it never existed, researchers from Great Britain and the United States took up the most advanced scientific instruments available. They combed the lake from one end to the other with cameras, sonar, and other detection devices. Yet despite all the investigation, the lake would not give up its monster.

In 1969, an American named Dan Taylor tried another way. Taylor built a submarine, which he christened the *Viperfish*, to plumb the depths of Loch Ness. Taylor worked alone and used his own money for what he called the "Nessa Project." He fitted the *Viperfish* with arc lights and photographic gear as well as an air gun. The gun would fire a retrievable dart that would take a small tissue sample of the monster for analysis.

The *Viperfish* expedition drew a little more attention than Taylor wanted. On July 16, 1969, the House of Lords, the upper house of the British Parliament, held a debate on the project. Some members had their suspicions about the intent of the submarine; others did not approve of Taylor's plan to sample a hunk of the monster's flesh. One member of the House of Lords, Lord Hughes, assured his peers that the hunt had only peaceful purposes and that no animals would be harmed by the research:

This technique is widely used for tagging whales. In the particular context of this scientific expedition I hardly think it constitutes damage or assault. . . . Unless and until the monster is found and examined we cannot even say whether the provisions of the Cruelty to Animals Act of 1876 would be relevant, since that Act does not apply to invertebrates.[15]

To date, the *Viperfish* has turned up no evidence of a plesiosaur or any other form of the Loch Ness monster. This has not discouraged Dan Taylor, who scheduled another expedition to Loch Ness in another submarine in the year 2002. As reporter Noel Young said of him, "Taylor is one of that very particular species of eccentrics, the Nessie hunter. Like UFO spotters and alien conspiracy theorists, they're obsessive

A large crane lowers the submarine Viperfish *into Loch Ness.*

Dan Taylor and the *Viperfish*

There is more than one way to search for the Loch Ness monster. Dan Taylor is still trying one of the most dangerous ways of all: an underwater search in a one-man submarine. Taylor first volunteered to bring the *Viperfish*, a twenty-foot, two-ton yellow submarine he had built himself, to Scotland to hunt for the Loch Ness monster in 1969. Unfortunately, the *Viperfish* found no evidence whatsoever for the monster.

Dan Taylor has not given up. He has prepared a second submarine, the forty-two-foot *Nessa*, for a second look at Loch Ness in 2002. This new submarine will be bigger and faster than the *Viperfish*, but its mission remains the same: to retrieve a tissue sample of the monster for scientific analysis.

by nature. He has spent a large part of his retirement savings, $200,000, building the submarine that will help him in his quest."[16]

The Persistent Robert Rines

The most persistent and optimistic Loch Ness investigator was Robert Rines, an American inventor and patent attorney who was also an expert in building and operating sonar equipment. Rines belonged to the Inventors' Hall of Fame; his sonar inventions helped find the sunken passenger liner *Titanic*. He also established his own law school, the Franklin Pierce Law Center, which specializes in patent and invention law. Rines did not need attention, notoriety, or fame and fortune. But Loch Ness intrigued him, and after hearing Roy Mackal's speech he dedicated himself to finding the elusive Loch Ness monster.

Rines knew that he would be ridiculed, but he did not mind. To him, science was much more than wearing a white coat and shuffling around a laboratory, teaching at a chalkboard, or making calculations in a notebook. Science, in his opinion, was simply the investigation of the natural world in all its forms, something that can be done just about anyplace, by anyone, and for any reason. The fact that most scientists made their living in strictly defined and limited professions did not make the search for unexplained creatures any less scientific.

Rines traveled to Loch Ness in 1970 with a new tool ready: side-scan sonar. Since photographs had not provided definitive proof that the Loch Ness monster existed, Rines and other researchers had decided to use sonar to scan the lake. Sonar is standard equipment on submarines, which need some detecting device to find their way around and to seek out the enemy in wartime. Underwater sonar equipment emits sound waves, which bounce off objects in the water and then can be received and read, giving a rough size and shape to any large moving object.

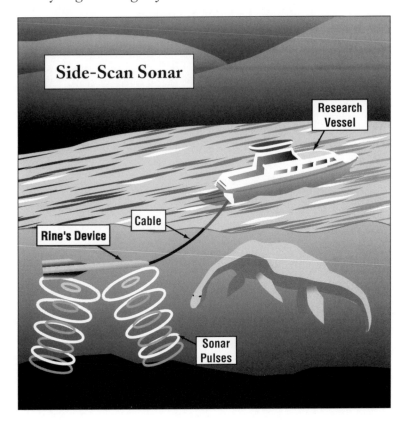

Side-Scan Sonar

Research Vessel

Cable

Rine's Device

Sonar Pulses

Sonar may find objects invisible to ordinary still or film cameras, which need light to function. When suspended from the side of a slowly moving boat, Rines's device was able to sweep the entire width of the lake with sonar pulses. The side-scan sonar can detect large or small moving objects in the water; it can also determine the location of underwater caves. While controlling the device from the boat, Rines studied a long, slowly moving sheet of graph paper, which showed the sonar contacts as marks made by a sensitive recording pen.

In its first season of use, the side-scan sonar detected several large moving objects. But Rines and his crew could not determine what exactly was showing up on the recording paper. Were they seeing a record of the Loch Ness monster, a large tree trunk, an otter, gas bubbles rising from the floor of the lake? They decided that a camera, as well as a light to penetrate the dark, peat-stained waters of the lake, was needed to assist in the search. In 1972, Rines returned to Loch Ness with a camera and a specially designed underwater strobe light created by Harold Egerton. When a sonar contact was made, the light flashed in coordination with the opening of the camera shutter. The camera (hopefully) would then take a picture of the object or animal that was causing the contact.

That summer, Rines caught his first glimpse of the Loch Ness monster. On June 23, while he was sipping tea with friends at their lakeside cottage, his wife shouted to him from the front porch. Rines rushed out. A large hump, rising about five feet from the water, swam away from the shore, turned, swam back, and disappeared. As Rines told a reporter, "The hair went up on the back of my neck. I'll never forget it as long as I live. My God, at that moment I knew there was something in there. I knew it was an animal!"[17]

That same year, aboard the Academy of Applied Science (AAS) expedition boat *Narwahl*, something else happened. Rines's sonar picked up a large moving object, and the strobe-

Robert Rines believed the Loch Ness monster was a plesiosaur.

linked camera snapped a picture. The picture showed a disturbance in the water, a flash of bubbles reflected by the light, and a faint, triangular object that measured about eight by four feet. It could have been a fin or a flipper. But it could also have been another trick of the water and the light.

Three years later, Rines and Charles Wyckoff had another stroke of luck. On the same day, about six hours apart, two photographs were taken, and in these pictures there seemed to be much more than a flipper flashing through the water. One photograph showed a bright oval shape extending into a long, narrow object that might be an animal's neck. The other picture was filled with an eerie, rough, and mottled object that looked like a gargoyle's head with a huge dark eye peering back at the viewer. Rines believed he had finally caught the Loch Ness monster on film. There was no longer any doubt in his mind: The Loch Ness monster was a plesiosaur, a species of ancient amphibian trapped and alive in the lake.

The two photographs gained much attention. The respectable science magazine *Nature* published them. Newspapers around the world ran the stories and the photographs, and scientists and experts convened meetings.

The Caledonian Canal

The Caledonian Canal plays a key role in many theories of what the Loch Ness monster might be. The canal was designed by Thomas Telford and begun in the early nineteenth century. It allowed small boats to sail from Dochgarroch, near Inverness, through Loch Ness, Loch Oich, and Loch Lochy. From one end of the Great Glen to another, the canal and the lakes stretch a distance of about sixty-six miles. At Inverness, a series of locks allow boats to climb the fifty-two feet needed to reach Loch Ness.

Some researchers believe that the canal allows sea dwellers such as eels, flounder, sturgeon, and seals to reach Loch Ness, a freshwater habitat they are not well adapted to. These species find the waters of Loch Ness too cold, too empty of prey, or perhaps too crowded with curious tourists and usually return to the North Sea the way they came. This frustrates scientists who are looking for an unknown native of the lake.

The Caledonian Canal as it appeared in the late 1800s.

Rines and Sir Peter Scott, a British scientist, planned a public symposium in Edinburgh, the largest city in Scotland, at which the final proof of the monster's existence would be presented to the public, and at which Rines could claim credit for the great discovery.

As in the 1930s after the first sighting by John Mackay and his wife, many people fully expected the mystery to be solved and science to provide an explanation for the miraculous. The world waited for Nessie to surface and make itself known, once and for all, and with no doubt whatsoever. In the June 1976 issue of *Smithsonian* magazine, John P. Wiley wrote,

> There's something in the loch, something big, even though we don't know what. It now seems likely that we will find out in the near future, and for some the knowledge will be a little saddening as well as fascinating. The mystery will be gone (as may be the unlamented promotions of tourist boards and whisky companies). The zoological record may be a little richer, but the world of our imaginations will be a little poorer.[18]

Convinced that something had to be done, the British Parliament organized a scientific symposium. There, the members of Parliament passed a law that protected the Loch Ness monster, whatever and wherever it was, from poaching. Sir Peter Scott also gave the monster its official scientific name: Nessiteras rhombopteryx, which means "diamond-finned Ness marvel."

At a meeting convened at the Smithsonian Institution in Washington, D.C., George R. Zug, the museum's curator of reptiles and amphibians, said, "I started as a skeptic. Now I believe there is a population of large animals in the loch. I don't have any idea of what they are; I have no way of identifying them. And I'm not going to try to identify them until I meet one eye to eye."[19]

Zug and other scientists were still not going to be convinced—not until they had evidence that would prove the Loch Ness monster beyond any doubt. Tourists and local residents believed what they wanted, while most people outside of Scotland found the Loch Ness monster to be little more than a funny story. Skeptics still made up the majority, and some very observant people pointed out that, when rearranged, the letters of Nessiteras rhombopteryx spelled "monster hoax by Sir Peter S."

The clouds of skepticism began to replace the hopeful optimism that had surrounded the efforts of the LNIB. As one leading doubter, naturalist Adrian Shine, put it, "By 1967 it was clear that something was wrong. The war of attrition against the law of averages seemed lost, yet the sightings record was undiminished. In human terms, the evidence for unusual creatures in the loch was overwhelming, yet photographic surveillance on the most massive and protracted scale could not produce verification."[20]

Fish Blood, Dolphins, and a Dinosaur

Nevertheless, Robert Rines would not give up. Hunting and finding the Loch Ness monster became an important part of his life's work, and he returned to the lake every summer to try something new. He was sure that, sooner or later, the Loch Ness monster would make its debut on the world's scientific stage, and he would win the honor, esteem, and long-lasting fame that comes to those who make important scientific discoveries.

Rines used every device and tried every method. In 1976, he gathered a team of more than twenty scientists and engineers, using sonar, 16-millimeter cameras, time-lapse photography, strobe lights, television cameras, infrared detectors, and a control room on shore. Hoping for a scoop, the *New York Times* sponsored the effort, and *National Geographic* magazine supplied teams of divers, photographers, and sonar experts, including Dr. Robert Ballard of the Woods Hole Oceanographic Institution (who would later win worldwide fame for his discovery of the *Titanic* wreck). Although more than 108,000 photographs were taken, they showed nothing—not so much as a salmon.

The 1976 summer expedition used many innovative tricks to bring Nessie to the surface. Containers of fish blood were trailed through the water, and the recorded sounds of fish in distress were broadcast, a technique that is often used to attract sharks. Light and sound were also flashed into the water to bring any curious amphibians to the surface.

The sonar equipment did pick up many unexpected objects, including bottles, shoes, tires, and "stone circles" raised by the ancient inhabitants of the Highlands. The expedition also spotted the remains of a navy flying boat that was ditched in Loch Ness during World War II. However, no proof of the Loch Ness monster was found.

Nevertheless, Robert Rines kept up the chase, with cameras, video equipment, and sonar. In the spirit of the inquiring scientist, he used all available methods to track down his elusive prey. In 1979, it was dolphins:

> The idea was that the dolphins, with their superb natural senses, would find the monster, at which point the strobes would illuminate and the cameras document its existence. But before the dolphins could be transported to Loch Ness, one of them died and Rines decided to cancel the attempt.[21]

Robert Rines (left) sets up a camera on the shore of Loch Ness.

Even after all of Rines's efforts, for most scientists, the proof still was not quite there. The long-necked creature in his photos could have been a gas bubble, the scaly head could have been the trunk of a submerged tree. There was still no body, no skin, no bones. Rines, many believed, had fallen victim to yet another trick of the eye, although a very good trick indeed.

The Skeptical Adrian Shine

Watching all the activity with intense interest was Adrian Shine, an Englishman who had been searching for the Loch Ness monster long before Robert Rines ever set foot in the Highlands. At one time, Shine had fervently believed that

Adrian Shine (left) searches for the Loch Ness monster every year.

there was something incredible to be discovered within Loch Ness. Every year, when the weather was good, he had launched some kind of searching expedition in the lake. Sometimes he went by himself, just to watch and wait. Sometimes he had a group with him, with cameras and binoculars at the ready. To get a closer look, he once built a small diving bell out of fiberglass. He lowered the craft thirty feet into the water, while an air hose ran to the surface and a bellows pumped air into the bell from the shore. From the small window of the bell, he spotted nothing but small fish and vegetation.

Shine could claim a sighting of his own. But his glimpse of the monster brought him to a very different conclusion than that of Robert Rines:

> It was a translucent calm just before a thunderstorm. Tranquilly, gently, a massive black hump came out from behind the headland. It was alive, it was moving, no question about it. I stopped. I took a photograph. I'd read the books—it was a classic sighting. I got my cinecamera ready for it to move again. I rowed slowly toward it. It then began to look much more like a massive head, flush with the surface, looking at me. I was alone. I was twelve miles away from the nearest habitation, but I rowed closer. And then I saw it was a rock—a rock that appeared to move owing to the motion of the boat.[22]

Although Shine had his doubts about the Loch Ness monster phenomenon, he did not give up the search. He used photographs, film cameras, and sonar, Robert Rines's specialty. Determined to search every corner of Loch Ness, Adrian Shine carried out Operation Deepscan on October 9–10, 1987. Twenty boats set out from Fort Augustus, each carrying the latest echo-sounding sonar equipment on board. The boats crossed the lake in a straight line, followed by a single, faster boat, christened the *New Atlantis*, which would move into place to more closely examine any unexplained contact that might occur.

Operation Deepscan hit three unexplained sonar contacts on the first day, one of them describing an object of about fifty pounds lying at a depth of about five hundred feet. Unfortunately, when the *New Atlantis* moved into position, it failed to discover anything—whatever the object had been, it had disappeared. The *New Atlantis* marked this position with navigational equipment. The next day, five boats searched the area but found nothing. Adrian Shine grew even more skeptical of the elusive plesiosaur. Believers assured themselves that the convoy had simply missed its target, which must be hiding in an underwater cave.

During Operation Deepscan, Shine did make what he considered to be a very important find when he pulled a thick, knobby tree stump from the bed of the lake. The

Shine's Operation Deepscan searched the entire lake using sonar and twenty boats.

stump bore a very strong resemblance to the gargoyle head in the 1975 photograph snapped by Robert Rines. To this day, the stump is on display at the Loch Ness Exposition in Drumnadrochit, Scotland, on the shores of Loch Ness. Visitors can decide for themselves: Was the face of the Loch Ness monster no more than an ugly tree?

Scientific Tricksters?

Rines and other scientists claim to be completely impartial in their search for the truth. Tampering with evidence, in any way, often makes that evidence useless. This is especially true when the evidence comes from photographs and film—media that can be easily altered to show what a skilled technician wants it to show.

Suspicion began swirling around the Rines "flipper" photographs when two engineers, Alan Kielar and Ricky Razdan, made their own sweep of the loch with sonar in 1983. Setting up 144 separate sonar emitters all over the lake, they calibrated the devices to set off an alarm any time the sonar detected an object larger than ten feet long. Months of waiting brought no result. Kielar and Razdan then took a closer look at the sonar contacts and photographs that Rines had made. While investigating how these photographs had been originally published in *Nature* and other print media, they discovered that the photos had been enhanced.

Kielar and Razdan learned that the flipper images were taken on August 8, 1972, with a 16-millimeter time-lapse camera. The camera was linked to a strobe light that was used to illuminate the murky water. Every forty-five seconds, the light went off, and the camera took a picture. On that day, the sonar equipment detected some large object in the water, and three frames of the film showed an unidentified object, which the researchers believed was the object that set off the sonar equipment.

The original images were faint. There was little to be seen except a blurry line, surrounded by what may have been

Alan Kielar reviews sonar readings (right) from sonar emitters that were placed throughout the lake (below).

bubbles or small bits of debris in the water. Rines and his partners in the Academy of Applied Sciences could not make out what the pictures showed, but they knew there were many different ways to clarify them. To enhance the photographs, the AAS researchers turned them over to Alan Gillespie, a student of geology who brought the images to the Jet Propulsion Laboratory in California. Gillespie used electronic equipment to scan the photos and enhance them.

To Rines and the AAS, Gillespie was simply applying modern means to help in the search. They believed that if a blurry photograph could be put in sharper focus, there was no reason not to do so. And the results of Gillespie's work did bring out a diamond shaped object in the water, an object whose size and appearance was comparable to the flipper of a plesiosaur.

To Kielar and Razdan, and to Loch Ness skeptics, however, it looked as if the AAS was tampering with evidence. Was Robert Rines's plesiosaur actually a "special effect" created by a team desperate to claim a discovery after many months of fruitless hard work? In 1984, some charged Rines with "retouching" the photos in order to bring out more clearly the appearance of a flipper. Robert Rines and Charles Wyckoff, the photographic expert who worked with the AAS, denied these charges. But they did admit that several published photographs were composites of different enhanced images. They also claimed that newspapers and magazines retouched the photographs on their own, making them more believable and more sensational for their readers.

So, what are the objects shown in these photographs? They may be the fin of an eel or a large salmon. In their articles about the mystery, Kielar and Razdan claim that the sonar contacts were made by large but ordinary objects such as boulders, tree trunks, and boats. Others believe that the fin may be some kind of vegetation or a trick of the underwater light.

Underwater Scanning

Although Robert Rines has been the individual most dedicated to it, many people have searched for the Loch Ness monster, and have used all kinds of ways to find it. Most simply watch from shore or from the deck of a boat. Actually getting into the lake poses an entirely different challenge. Not only is the lake very cold, but it is also very dark. Any diver that descends more than a few feet will discover daylight rapidly weakening. At a very shallow depth, Loch Ness turns black, and even a skilled diver can lose all sense of direction and have a hard time finding the way back to the surface.

While the debate over the Loch Ness monster raged on, the sightings continued. Two locals gave the following testimony to a television crew from the United States:

> It was just big, I think that's the best way to put it. So it certainly wasn't a seal and it certainly wasn't a fish.

Exploring Loch Ness underwater is dangerous since it turns pitch black at a shallow depth and is extremely cold.

And all I can say is, looking at the Loch, is that somewhere in there is the Loch Ness Monster, and as far as I'm concerned, I've seen it.

I saw it and I'm not going to be dissuaded. I know, and it wasn't just, you know, an imagination, and I'm a sane guy. I've got no axe to grind. As I say, I sell pet food. What use to me is the Loch Ness Monster?[23]

Still, there is no evidence for the Loch Ness monster apart from questionable film, photographs, sonar readings, and eyewitness sightings. There is no physical evidence—no bodies and no bones. No monster corpses have floated to shore. None have been caught in nets, or have taken a baited hook, or been trapped on land. There are no skeletons or fossils that might put a scientific name to a long-necked amphibian, with or without flippers, that might be leading a secretive life through the depths of Loch Ness.

Chapter 4

Plesiosaur Possibilities

By the end of the twentieth century, dozens of expeditions to Loch Ness had been organized by universities, research institutes, museums, and individuals who took a strong interest in the subject of the Loch Ness monster. Searchers used every device they could think of to scan the lake from one end to the other. Thousands of feet of film had been examined, and miles of graph paper had been analyzed for telltale shapes and sounds. But nobody found convincing evidence of Nessie's existence. The Loch Ness monster has turned out to be one of the most elusive quarries ever pursued by modern science. In the twenty-first century, the mystery remains.

Although physical evidence is lacking, the searchers have produced dozens of theories about the Loch Ness mystery. One theory stubbornly persists among many experts: The Loch Ness monster is a prehistoric dinosaur, perhaps a species of plesiosaur, a family of long-necked amphibians thought to be extinct. Somehow, this plesiosaur survived the mass extinction 65 million years ago and lives today in the murky waters of the lake, surviving on scarce resources and eluding all attempts to trap it.

As Steuart Campbell explains, the plesiosaur theory goes all the way back to the middle of the nineteenth century:

As early as 1859 Philip Gosse popularized the plesiosaur as an explanation for the mystery of the sea

Some experts theorize that the Loch Ness monster is a dinosaur that somehow survived to the present day.

serpent. Folklore thus modernized itself to the findings of science. When [writer Rupert] Gould explained [Nessie] as a lake-locked sea serpent it was inevitable that the former would then be regarded as a plesiosaur. This notion has been particularly persistent, despite the lack of evidence for sea serpents, or the implausibility of Gould's hypothesis (that a sea serpent had somehow traveled unseen up the River Ness).[24]

The name plesiosaur means "near lizard," because the first plesiosaur skeleton that was discovered looked like a giant lizard. Scientists generally agree that plesiosaurs lived about 230 million years ago, during the late Triassic period. They evolved at the same time as nothosaurs, amphibious creatures with webbed feet that could travel on land or in the water. There were many different kinds of prehistoric swimming reptiles, such as the ichthyosaur, which looked like a large dolphin with feet. Rather than feet, however, plesiosaurs had paddles or flippers, which allowed them to glide easily over long distances at sea. Some plesiosaurs had long necks and small skulls; others had large skulls and short necks. They ranged in length from two meters to about twenty-two meters.

There are still many mysteries surrounding the plesiosaurs. Most plesiosaur finds consist of only a few bones or teeth. Scientists are not sure how they bred—whether by laying eggs or by giving birth to live young. They lived along seacoasts and in sheltered bays and estuaries, but they also may have lived in the open ocean.

A few things regarding the plesiosaurs are certain. First, they lived alongside the dinosaurs through the Jurassic and Cretaceous periods. Plesiosaur bones and fossils have been found all over the world, and in much the same condition as the remains of extinct dinosaurs such as the allosaurus or the stegosaurus. Second, most scientists also agree that plesiosaurs suffered the same fate as the dinosaurs, dying out in a mysterious mass extinction that took place about 65 million years ago.

A major problem with the theory that the Loch Ness monster is a surviving plesiosaur is that very few paleontologists accept it. In the world of paleontologists—men and

An ichthyosaur (left) and a plesiosaur, prehistoric creatures that have fueled speculation about the origins of the Loch Ness monster.

women who study the life-forms of prehistory—the Loch Ness monster is something slightly embarrassing, like an old joke that has been told too many times. Nevertheless, survivors from the age of the dinosaurs abound. There are species of reptiles walking or crawling the earth today that lived at the same time as the bony-plated stegosaurus and the towering allosaurus. Many insect species that flew about in those times still exist, biting, scratching, annoying, and alarming humans today. But none of these survivors are large, long-necked amphibians.

The Surprising Coelacanth

Still, Loch Ness believers have not given up on the plesiosaur theory. They hold out hope because on one occasion, a long-extinct fish did come back to life in the waters of the Indian Ocean. It happened in 1938, as the trawler *Nerine* was sailing off the coast of southern Africa, its nets out and crew watching in curiosity as a strange, bluish, five-foot-long fish, with four pairs of fins, was hauled onto the deck. The fish resembled no fish they had ever caught before.

The skipper of the *Nerine*, Hendrik Goosen, could make no use of the fish, as he had no idea what it was, and it did not seem to be an edible species. He brought it ashore and sold it to a South African woman who sometimes bought his more curious castoffs.

The buyer, Marjorie Courtney-Latimer, a curator of the East London Museum in South Africa, could not identify the fish. She wrote a letter to Professor James Smith, a chemistry professor who made a hobby out of ichthyology, the scientific study and classification of fish. From the drawing and the description, Professor Smith thought he recognized the fish, but he could not be sure until he saw it.

When Smith finally did see the fish, he began trembling with amazement. There was no doubt about it: He was looking at a coelacanth (SEE-la-kanth). At the time, the coelacanth was thought to be extinct. It was supposed to have died

off with the dinosaurs at the end of the Cretaceous period, about 65 million years ago. After this discovery, hunting the coelacanth in the Indian Ocean became a favorite sport of ichthyologists. Ship captains and fishermen were alerted to be on the lookout for a long, blue, four-finned fish, and generous rewards were offered for its capture.

When a skeptic denies the possibility that the Loch Ness monster could be a survivor from the age of the dinosaurs, believers cite the amazing "rediscovery" of the coelacanth. Skeptics like Richard Frere have an argument ready:

> The coelacanth is a fish, not a reptile. Because it was only known for a long time by its fossil remains it was thought to be extinct. . . . Living in an unchanging environment, it was able to survive with a minimum of evolutionary adjustment.

> The plesiosaur was a reptile, not a fish. Like all reptiles it was cold blooded and if, to make a hypothetical point, a live member of the order were introduced into Loch Ness's water at a temperature of 5–6 degrees Celsius, it would rapidly die or else go into a state of hibernation.[25]

Believers in the Loch Ness monster are not persuaded by this argument. They point out that scientists and experts have often been wrong in the past. Scientists have not discovered everything the natural world has to offer, they say, and they will certainly be surprised again in the future.

Long Necks in Loch Ness?

For many years, the plesiosaur remained the most common explanation for the sightings in Loch Ness. The appearance of plesiosaurs, which had oval bodies, long necks, and flippers, seemed to fit well with the descriptions of Nessie and its cousins in North America. The skeletons of plesiosaurs also seemed to fit with the images taken underwater by Robert Rines, who captured a "fin" in his two famous photographs of Loch Ness taken in 1972. The long neck in the 1975 Rines photograph also seemed to match the appearance of the unidentified creature in the "surgeon's photograph" of 1934.

But how did a plesiosaur show up in this lake? A species of plesiosaur, believers say, could have entered the Great Glen region and inhabited Loch Ness in prehistoric times. At some point, the lake was cut off from the sea, and a population of plesiosaurs was trapped. This could have happened during the last ice age, for example, when a glacier filling the glen gradually retreated to the northeast, leaving behind a deep valley that turned an arm of the sea into a landlocked, freshwater lake.

The survivors could also have entered the loch through an underwater tunnel or stream that at one time linked the Great Glen with the open sea. The tunnel theory is helped by the fact that the bottom and sides of Loch Ness are practically invisible to still photographs and film. Researchers still have not surveyed and mapped every corner of the deep lake, and new underwater caverns have been discovered by sonar surveys.

According to these theories, the plesiosaur of Loch Ness escaped whatever phenomenon brought about the mass extinction of the dinosaurs. Many scientists believe that this extinction resulted from a comet or asteroid impact that occurred in the vicinity of the Yucatán Peninsula, in what is now Mexico, about 65 million years ago. This impact must have thrown an immense amount of debris and dust into the atmosphere, which in turn caused the earth to cool and much of its vegetation to die out. Many scientists believe that there is a direct link between the extinction of the dinosaurs and this drastic cooling of the earth's climate. Could a plesiosaur already living in a cold region tough out the sudden global winter that occurred?

There are a few problems with the theory of the trapped plesiosaur as a cold-weather survivor. First, the dinosaur extinction that occurred was a worldwide phenomenon. Whatever happened to the dinosaurs happened to all of them, no matter where or how they lived. Although insects, reptiles, and fish survived, no dinosaurs did. If there were such creatures in the vicinity of Loch Ness, there should be some fossil remains of dinosaurs in the rock and sediments surrounding the lake, but there are none—or at least, none have been found.

Dinosaur fossils have never been found in the region of Loch Ness.

Nessie's Lair

On November 30, 1989, George Edwards, an auxiliary member of Her Majesty's Coastguard and the skipper of the cruise boat *Nessie Hunter,* made an important discovery that has shaken up the world of Loch Ness research.

While taking part in an emergency exercise near Urquhart Castle, Edwards noticed a depth reading of 787 feet—37 feet more than normal in that part of the lake. Trolling farther around the area, Edwards recorded an even greater depth: 812 feet, deeper than any known part of Loch Ness. The depth might have indicated a cavern or an underwater trench that had never been recorded. Not wanting the celebrity that often came with dis-

coveries at Loch Ness, Edwards kept the information to himself. But eight years later, a friend relayed his story to a journalist, and within days the news of "Nessie's Lair" was appearing in newspapers all over the world.

Many Loch Ness experts consider Nessie's Lair to be very important in the search for the monster. If the 812-foot depth reading reveals an underwater cave, such a cave might be providing the beast of Loch Ness, whatever it is, with shelter from the prying eyes of photographers, scientists, sonar scanners, and tourists. It also may be the reason why sonar sweeps of the lake have failed to show any large animal underneath the surface.

Areas of great depth have been recorded in Loch Ness near Urquhart Castle.

Also, as a cold-blooded reptile, it seems unlikely that the plesiosaur could survive in the cold waters of Loch Ness. The water would prove to be a very hostile environment for a cold-blooded animal, which would either die out or search for a warmer habitat.

The survival of a family of plesiosaurs in a region not known for dinosaur remains seems unlikely. Plesiosaurs lived in tropical regions, and according to the fossil evidence, they died out with the rest of the dinosaurs. If a plesiosaur survived in a cold lake, then others should have been able to thrive in warmer waters as well. But no modern plesiosaur has ever been found in any climate.

Most scientists are also skeptical about any surviving dinosaur reaching Loch Ness through an underground tunnel linking the lake to the sea. The surface of Loch Ness lies sixteen meters above sea level, and if such a tunnel existed it would drain the lake to sea level. There is no evidence that shows that Loch Ness was ever connected to the sea. In addition, the Highlands of Scotland underwent heavy glaciation in the last ice age (ten thousand years ago); this would probably have driven any surviving dinosaur species far to the south.

In a *National Geographic* article summing up the big 1976 expedition of Loch Ness, author William S. Ellis wrote,

> Those who say the plesiosaur has survived and is alive and well in the loch are flying in the face of some steely missiles of scientific data. The plesiosaur, an air-breathing marine dinosaur, dates back more than 200 million years. It is believed to have vanished about 65 million years ago. . . . Let it be allowed that when the black curtain of extinction fell on that blimpish beast, one—no, it would have to be at least two—may have survived. But surely, the glacier that moved through the loch ended any such miracle of endurance.[26]

Other Problems

Any newly discovered species would be a great achievement for zoologists. Does the Loch Ness monster fall into a category of unseen, unlikely, but very real species of monster, such as the coelacanth? There are some problems with this theory as well. First, Loch Ness is a very cold lake; its temperature averages about 42 degrees Fahrenheit. If an amphibian somehow reached the lake after the last ice age, it seems unlikely that such a creature would find Loch Ness a very comfortable place to live.

Then again, animals can adapt, and some mammals and amphibian species survive well in a cold environment. But there is another problem with Loch Ness: a lack of food. The peat from the surrounding hills drains into Loch Ness during frequent rains. This peat makes the lake cloudy, and because light penetrates only a few feet, the lake has a shortage of the light-nourished plankton that small fish feed on. Because these small fish, which occupy the bottom steps of the food chain, must struggle to survive, they are few in number. Thus, a population of large amphibians in the lake would find it very difficult to survive on the scarce food resources. Likely, they would be forced to come ashore to do their hunting, so there would be many more sightings of the beasts by passing cars and pedestrians.

In their report presented at the Edinburgh conference, Rines and Scott provided this retort to those arguing that a large amphibian could not survive on the resources of Loch Ness:

> The "population density" of the Nessies is no doubt dictated by the size of the loch and the abundance of food. . . . Salmon, sea trout and elvers [young, migrating eels] running up the River Ness into the loch can thereafter swim up a number of rivers which run into it, and salmon, sea trout and well-grown eels must descend these rivers into the loch on their way

back to the sea. There are also resident populations of brown trout, char and sticklebacks. The shallow waters are well grown with freshwater weeds, and organic detritus must also be considered as a possible food source.[27]

Rines and Scott also considered the fact that Nessies were so rarely sighted:

Reptiles must breathe air, though comparatively infrequently. A terrapin has been recorded as surviving one year of continuous submersion. Should the nessies wish to breathe quite frequently, they would not be detected easily if the nostrils were at the topmost point to break surface. Many accounts of head sightings speak of "horns" or "ears" which may be extensions of the nostrils into breathing tubes. With

This photograph, taken in May 1977, seems to support the existence of the Loch Ness monster.

any ripple on the water it would not be difficult for a Nessie to breathe undetected. In flat calm conditions, the surface is constantly dimpled by rising fish, and again the animal would be likely to go unnoticed.[28]

The two still had difficulty convincing others of the Loch Ness monster, no matter how scientifically possible it was. They still had no evidence that would prove their theories. They could not duplicate their findings—a vital part of scientific proof—by capturing similar sonar readings or video images several times. They had no body and no bones, no hair or teeth. Eventually, they put an end to their expeditions and began considering the possibility that the incredible Loch Ness monster was no more than a garden-variety folktale.

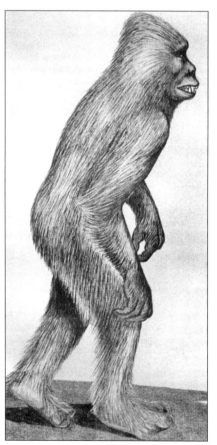

The yeti, like the Loch Ness monster, is rumored to exist—but no one knows for sure.

Peering at the Water

Loch Ness is not the only place where unseen creatures are said to lurk. Rumors and stories of monsters are told in every corner of the globe. In the Himalayan Mountains of Asia, the elusive yeti, or abominable snowman, is said to roam the slopes. The yeti resembles a man but is not a modern human. Instead, it is thought to be a survivor from an earlier age of human development—possibly a Neanderthal.

Some Australians believe in a tiger that roams the outback, the region of hot, scrubby desert that covers much of the country's interior. The people of the European Alps fear the tatzelwurm, a huge lizard. A huge wolf is said to roam the Andes Mountains of South America. In Lake Storsjön, in the mountains of central Sweden, lives the Storsjo monster, seen by many local fishermen and farmers. The Native Americans of British Columbia tell of the Ogopogo, a lake monster that inhabits Lake Okanagan.

Steven Feltham's Nessie-Sery Research

The search for the Loch Ness monster brings all kinds of people to the shores of the lake. Some are just tourists, hoping for a drive through a beautiful countryside and the chance for a glimpse of a mystery. Others arrive but never leave, and dedicate their lives to the hunt. One of these is Steven Feltham.

Feltham lives in a small van on the shore of Loch Ness. Near the van is the sign of his one-man search organization: Nessie-sery Research. Feltham spends most of his time with high-powered binoculars and a film camera in search of the image that will finally convince everyone that the Loch Ness monster exists. He is confident that as technology improves, the Loch Ness

monster will be discovered. As quoted in an Internet article, he explains,

> The way I see it, this is such a small country we're living in and we now understand just about every inch of it. Well, this is something we don't have an explanation for.
>
> I'm open-minded, but I think there are 20 to 30 of them in there. . . . Technology will move on another stage eventually and we'll be able to look through the water and see what there is. This is the biggest shop window in the world. Zoologists will one day come and say "Oh well, I thought that all along."

Steven Feltham lives in his van near Loch Ness and waits to capture an image of the Loch Ness monster.

Those who visit Loch Ness today are well aware of the monster legend, which has been spread all over the world in books, articles, and television shows. A person driving or hiking along Loch Ness peers carefully at the water, eager for a look at the paddling plesiosaur. Sightings also can be inspired by word of mouth, for it seems that once a look at Loch Ness is published in the local papers, the number of sightings sharply rises.

But in his book *Loch Ness Monster: The Evidence*, Steuart Campbell points out another interesting fact about Ness watching: The more people that are sent to watch and search the lake, the fewer sightings there are:

> This is what would be expected if [Nessie] does not exist. If reports are merely due to misinterpretation of the commonplace at distances too great to allow proper identification and/or by inexperienced observers, then saturating the surroundings with skilled observers is bound to reduce or even eliminate reports of [Nessie]. The skilled observer sees what the unskilled sees, but he knows that it is not [Nessie] and does not report it.[29]

Nevertheless, there have been startling sightings by the most rational of beings—twentieth century scientists—and these events have turned skeptics into agnostics, and then into believers. There are pictures, films, and sonar readings of a large and swiftly moving object on and under the lake. If there is no monster and no plesiosaur, what could the explanation be?

Chapter 5

Other Explanations

In the view of most scientists, the Loch Ness monster falls into the same category as Ogopogo and the Storsjo monster. It is nothing more than a local legend that has endured into the twenty-first century. It has been helped along by newspapers, by gullible tourists, and by the people of the Highlands, who seek to attract visitors to their region by spreading tall tales.

Yet many reliable eyewitness sightings remain. Scientists usually doubt such sightings, but they must. The business of science is verifiable evidence, unbiased investigation, and experiments that can be duplicated. Scientists cannot use eyewitness reports, or rumors, or speculative articles that run in newspapers. And as far as they can tell, most of the natural world on Earth has been seen and described already.

It is also the scientist's job to explain, however, and many scientists have offered plausible explanations for the happenings at Loch Ness. The explanations run the gamut, from the sighting of common species such as deer, large fish, or otters to strange weather and wind effects and mass delusion. These scientific explanations account for many sightings on Loch Ness, yet not one of them seems to account for all of them. Could there be several different explanations, each of them possible, reasonable, and logical?

Survivors from the Past

Several times in the past, legendary monsters have turned out to be normal living and breathing animals. During the exploration of the Pacific Ocean and the East Indies, European sailors had many unbelievable adventures and many tall tales to bring home. One such tale described a giant dragon that weighed several hundred pounds, ran as fast as a human, and could catch and kill any ordinary sized mammal, including a European sailor. For a long time, the lizard remained a sort of tropical Loch Ness monster—until a reptile pretty well fitting the description was caught in 1912 on the island of Komodo. This species grew up to twelve feet long, weighed as much as three hundred pounds, and had extremely powerful jaws and teeth that could be fatal to anyone unlucky enough to cross its path. Nowadays, nobody doubts the existence of the Komodo dragon.

The Komodo dragon was the subject of tall tales until it was discovered that the animal was real.

In Africa, a place where some regions are still unexplored by outsiders, people often spoke about a seemingly impossible animal that had a long neck, a mulelike body, a striped hide, and cloven hoofs. At the beginning of the twentieth century, zoologists heard about this mammal, called an okapi, and scoffed. Then Sir Harry Johnston left England for a journey into the Congo Free State. He heard about the okapi at many villages along his route. In 1901, while nearing exhaustion after a long, dangerous, and fruitless expedition, Johnston finally caught up with the okapi. It was real, all right: the closest living relative to the giraffe, lying freshly killed in a small village. The dead specimen was skinned, and its skull preserved. Johnston brought the remains back to skeptical Europe, and in honor of his quest, the okapi was given the scientific name Okapia johnstoni.

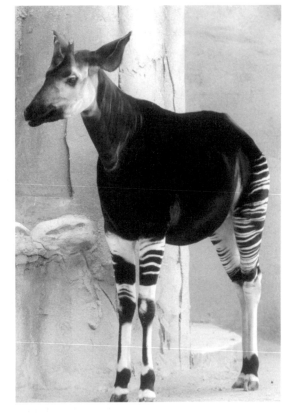

Some animals like the okapi are so unusual that many people thought they could not possibly be real.

The Mirage Monster?

Johnston and other scientists must search for explanations for whatever is witnessed, photographed, filmed, or recorded on a sonar tape. Accompanying the eyewitness sightings at Loch Ness have been many unexplainable occurrences documented in other media over the years. What could the explanation for this much better evidence be? One possibility is the ordinary atmospheric mirage.

Air, water, and temperature can affect objects seen at a distance in many different ways. Warm air rises; cold air sinks; a rapid change of temperature may turn an ordinary log or surface ripple into something much more menacing.

Cryptozoology

The discovery of the okapi and other unknown species gave rise to a new branch of the natural sciences known as cryptozoology. The term was invented in the 1950s by Bernard Heuvelmans, an author and researcher who many consider to be the "Father of Cryptozoology." "Cryptids" are unknown or legendary animals, as well as species thought by scientists to be extinct. In the search for cryptids, a cryptozoologist uses any and all means available: photography, sonar, satellite imaging, tracking, eyewitness reports, and legends.

Bigfoot, the Loch Ness monster, the "Champ" monster of Lake Champlain, and the yeti are among the more famous specimens known and studied by cryptozoologists. There are many more cryptids that are less famous, including the rock rats of Australia, the Myakka skunk ape of central Florida, the Japanese wolf, and the Beast of Bodmin Moore, a large cat—perhaps a puma—that many believe is roaming southern England.

Bigfoot, supposedly captured in this photo, is one of the more famous specimens studied by cryptozoologists.

Anyone driving or riding in a car can see such a mirage on a hot day when water or waves seem to rise from a distant field or road surface. Desert dwellers know that, no matter what their eyes tell them, there is no water in the distant sands. Are such mirages fooling monster hunters on Loch Ness?

Loch Ness has some geography in common with several other areas home to legendary monsters. (Lake monsters are also well known in Canada, the northern United States, Iceland, Scandinavia, and southern Argentina.) Loch Ness lies at an extreme temperate latitude and is surrounded by steep hills. In such a lake, and in the spring and early summer, it is common for the water temperature to be much lower than the air temperature. When this happens, a "temperature inversion" occurs, and objects can be seen to move as the air rises, falls, and moves about. Most of the Loch Ness sightings occurred under these conditions. Researcher W.H. Lehn witnessed this occurrence firsthand during his research in Canada:

> I have observed and photographed numerous mirages on Lakes Manitoba and Winnipeg. One of the observations was made by chance while swimming in Lake Manitoba on a hot day (7 August 1976); a thin horizontal black strip appeared on the surface of the lake for a few minutes, at an apparent distance of 1 or 2 km. Experience dictated that the observation be attributed to atmospheric refraction, but very little help from the imagination would have been required to interpret the shape as a long black serpent.[30]

Researchers also point out that almost nine out of ten Loch Ness sightings occur when the lake is "flat calm," or when there is no wind and no waves. Local people know this as "Nessie weather." Flat calm conditions are the best for making distant observations, but they are also best for atmospheric mirages. As Lehn points out,

> Many of the sightings involve observer elevations close to the level of the lake itself with the observer near the shore or in a boat. The distances along the line of sight are often of the order of 1 km or more. Either or both of these conditions require low, nearly

horizontal light rays to pass from object to observer. Exactly these rays are most easily (and noticeably) deflected by refractive anomalies in the air.[31]

Many other kinds of mirages may also be interpreted as a glimpse of a lake monster. A sudden rising wave may be caused by earth tremors that are weak enough to pass unnoticed on dry land. Windrows—dark regions created by the interaction of water and light at certain times of day—may be seen at a distance as long, dark, swiftly moving, unidentifiable shapes. Boat wakes can set up complex patterns of interference, creating humped waves on the surface of calm waters. The steep shores of the lake can reflect wakes back toward their point of origin, causing strange water disturbances long after a boat has passed. The same phenomenon can also occur underwater, as the sides of the banks reflect vague echoes that appear and disappear, fooling detection devices into displaying an image interpreted as an animal.

Many Loch Ness monster sightings seem to occur from platforms and other locations near or on the water.

Waves and boat wakes can do many strange and startling things to observers, whether they are out on the lake or watching from the shore. When a boat changes direction or stops suddenly, an interference pattern is set up between the outgoing wake and a new set of waves created by the new speed and direction of motion. The result, at times, is a "standing wave," a large, three-dimensional rise of water that can resemble the hump of a large animal, and which gradually recedes back to the surface, as if the animal had submerged or swam away. In some cases, the standing wave can endure for several minutes and, on occasion, long past the time when the boat that caused it has left the area. Standing waves may be the explanation for many sightings on the loch, especially when the honest observer claims that there was no boat anywhere to be seen.

One more possibility came to light in 1984, after many years of study by the Loch Ness Project, led by Adrian Shine. The project revealed that underwater waves might have accounted for the underwater sonar contacts. These waves are created by a thermocline, or boundary between very cold, deep water and warmer water lying closer to the surface. When a prevailing southwest wind blows the warmer layer to the north, the cold water rises behind it, creating turbulence. "When this happens," Adrian Shine reports, "objects on the surface such as logs can be borne along against the wind looking just like swimming animals. Underwater, huge waves form on the thermocline. The one measured in 1985 was 40 meters high. They are invisible at the surface but make gigantic sonar traces."[32]

The Loch Ness monster may also be attributed to an ordinary case of pareidolia. The Spicers, the Mackays, and all other witnesses to the Loch Ness monster may have fallen victim to this strange but common trick of their eyes. When the eye focuses on an object that it does not recognize, it searches through a memory bank of images and concepts,

Adrian Shine's sonar boat on Loch Ness. Shine's research suggests that sonar contacts made underwater might really be waves.

trying to match one with the object in view. The curving strap of a purse, lying just ten yards away, may turn into an idle black snake resting on the ground. A tree stump, seen through the dense branches and leaves of a forest, may be seen as a sleeping bear. Puffy clouds, shaped by the wind, form themselves into faces and animals. Otters that just climbed out of a cold lake in the late afternoon may look like prehistoric monsters.

As writer and skeptic Robert Todd Carroll explains in "The Skeptic's Dictionary,"

> Pareidolia is a type of illusion or misperception involving a vague or obscure stimulus being perceived as something clear and distinct. For example, in the discolorations of a burnt tortilla one sees the face of Jesus Christ. Or one sees the image of Mother Theresa in a cinnamon bun or the face of a man in the moon.
>
> Under ordinary circumstances, pareidolia provides a psychological explanation for many delusions based upon sense perception. For example, it explains many UFO sightings and hearing sinister messages on

records played backwards. Pareidolia explains Elvis, Bigfoot, and Loch Ness Monster sightings. It explains numerous apparitions and visions.[33]

Floating Objects, Dead and Alive

Another possible explanation for the Loch Ness monster is that it is a floating object, such as a tree trunk, a heavy branch, an oil drum, or a mat of vegetation, that suddenly rises from the bottom of the lake to the surface. Some sightings may be animals such as geese flying close to the surface, ordinary fish, or otters swimming underwater. Otters are excellent swimmers that can dive more than fifty feet deep and submerge for three minutes. They can grow to an impressive size but are quite shy of humans.

The otter theory was put forward by Maurice Burton, a zoologist from the British Museum who explained his take on the Loch Ness phenomenon in a book titled *The Elusive Monster*. Burton and many scientists claim that monster sightings in Loch Ness are really otters seen at a distance and under poor sighting conditions. Small roe deer, a species that

According to some scientists, an otter seen from a distance under poor visibility conditions is often mistaken for the Loch Ness monster.

can also swim, may also be mistaken for Nessie. Roe deer sport antlers that strongly resemble the elongated neck of a plesiosaur. Is the neck of the Loch Ness monster actually the antlers of an innocent deer, plunging into the water in flight from a camera-wielding tourist or paranormal investigator?

Another possibility is that there are indeed unusual visitors to Loch Ness from time to time. These visitors arrive from the North Sea via the River Ness. Porpoises and whales, for example, are large, strong underwater swimmers that must come to the surface to breathe from time to time. A black, shiny-skinned porpoise breaching the surface, blowing out air, and then diving back underwater can be a very startling sight, especially when it appears in a place that it is not supposed to be. Seals may also account for some Loch Ness sightings. Seals live near water, but they can move quickly on land. A seal swimming rapidly near the surface could be taken for something much larger than it really is. A gray seal was the conclusion offered by Sir Edward Mountain after his twenty-man lookout on Loch Ness in 1934.

Many more possibilities exist. The Loch Ness monster may be a walrus, a giant sea turtle, or a giant salamander. Or it may be a sturgeon, which can grow to a length of nearly ten feet and which sometimes reaches the rivers and bays of Great Britain from its natural habitat in the open sea. Because sturgeons do not breed in rivers, they would spend only a short time inland before returning to the open sea—leaving behind an unexplained mystery to anyone who might spot one swimming near the surface.

Bubbles from the Bottom

Since Loch Ness lies along a geologic fault line, it is home to some uncomfortable surprises in the form of earthquakes, tremors, and the like. Geologist Luigi Piccardi believes that such disturbances lie behind the sightings of the Loch Ness monster, and many other unexplained phenomena all over the

The Sightings Go On

Loch Ness monster sightings are not a thing of the past. Every year, a few people report something unusual they have spotted on the lake or on the roads and pastures that surround it. The latest such events are given on the Official Loch Ness Monster Fan Club website (www.lochness.co.uk/fan_club/thisyr.html #2001).

January 10, 2001

Dougie Barbour from Glasgow took pictures of a wake moving against the current from a layby [road turnout] near the Clansman Hotel during the mid-afternoon.

May 5, 2001

James Gray from Invermoriston took a series of five pictures showing a head and neck coming out of the water near the Invermoriston bay. The creature was about 30 meters from this boat and quickly disappeared below the surface of the water.

August 5, 2001

An Aberdeen man was watching the loch from Fort Augustus at around 9 P.M. He saw a large black form rise from the water and remain visible for around 5 seconds. A smaller black hump then appeared close to the first before disappearing.

world. Piccardi's explanation was given in a *San Francisco Chronicle* article titled "Mystery Unlocked?":

> Piccardi bases his theory on the fact that Loch Ness sits atop the Great Glen Fault, an active fault that slices through the Scottish Highlands surrounding the lake.
>
> His research reveals that Nessie sightings closely follow the rumblings of the fault. He believes the quakes inspired the first stories of the beast among the Picts, the ancient Scottish tribes known for their tattoos and for carved stone images of the monster. Piccardi also notes that the first written reference to

Nessie appears in a sixth-century manuscript that describes the life of St. Columba and refers to a dragon that arrives "with strong shaking" and leaves "shaking herself."[34]

Hoaxes

The mystery of Loch Ness is made more complicated by hoaxes. Many experts taking a good, close look at the Loch Ness photographs suspect that some of them are fakes. On many occasions, the Loch Ness monster has been a kind of national practical joke played by hoaxers and their trick photographs. Since everyone knows the legend of Loch Ness, a few among the observers go there simply to fool the gullible, see their names in the newspaper, and have a bit of fun.

In April 1994, another hoax came to light when journalists David Martin and Alastair Boyd claimed the famous "surgeon's photograph" depicted a model built and floated by Christian Spurling, the stepson of Marmeduke Wetherall. Martin and Boyd claimed that Wetherall may have been seeking revenge for a hoax played on him by a local man, who had pressed the bottom of an elephant-hoof umbrella stand into the earth near Loch Ness to fool what had been Wetherall's serious quest for the Loch Ness monster. By this theory, Wetherall had attached Spurling's dinosaur model to a toy submarine, submerged the contraption, and then enlisted Dr. R.K. Wilson, a surgeon with a doctor's good reputation, to pose it for a series of photographs somewhere in shallow water. Further adding to the mystery were two conflicting dates for the "surgeon's photograph": Wilson originally told the *London Daily Mail* he took the picture on April 19, 1934, while Rupert Gould gave the date as April 1, "All Fool's Day" in Great Britain, in his book *The Loch Ness Monster*.

Then again, the story of the hoax may have been a hoax itself. One of Wilson's photographs showed the same unidentified object sunk lower in the water. In the first photograph, circular rings appeared around the object—rings that could only have been created if it had popped up from beneath the surface.

Whatever it was, Wilson would not say. He kept away from reporters and kept the secret of his famous pictures completely to himself until the day he died in 1969. To those contemplating the existence of the Loch Ness monster, the surgeon's photograph remains a talisman, a powerful symbol of the mystery. Depending on one's opinion of the mystery, the photo may show the head and neck of the Loch Ness monster, the tail of an otter, or a practical joke.

The Monster: A Publicity Stunt?

There could be an even simpler explanation for the modern Loch Ness mystery. Author Henry H. Bauer, in his book *The Enigma of Loch Ness*, reports an interesting correspondence with "Lester Smith," the pseudonym of a fellow author who

A photograph taken in 1933 purportedly shows the Loch Ness monster.

wrote several volumes on mysterious and unexplained phenomena. Smith reveals that the Loch Ness monster was invented by him and two partners at a London publicity agency. For the sum of fifty pounds, paid by a group of hotel owners, the group was hired to find some way to promote tourism in the Highlands. The result was the famous sighting of the Loch Ness monster in 1933, according to Smith's testimony:

> [One of the partners] told us that for centuries a legendary creature was supposed to dwell in Loch Ness. We had never heard of it. At that time our "board room" was the saloon bar of a pub just off Trafalgar Square and over several pints of beer we became midwives of the reborn Loch Ness Monster. All we had to do was to arrange for the Monster to be sighted. This we did and the story snowballed. Thousands went north to see it and see it they did. It was, of course, pure hokum.[35]

Did Smith's group actually arrange the sighting of the Loch Ness monster by Mr. and Mrs. Mackay, managers of the Drumnadrochit Hotel, and inspire the newspaper articles that brought the Loch Ness monster and the Scottish Highlands to national attention? Were the hundreds of scientists and monster hunters who prowled the lake and its shores for the next six decades actually chasing a publicity stunt dreamed up over a few beers in a London pub? Mr. and Mrs. Mackay never admitted such, and there the story ends.

Yearning for the Incredible

There is nothing as fascinating to the human mind as the unknown. In ancient times, before scientific explanations were readily available, people did not know why natural phenomena such as storms, earthquakes, floods, and volcanic eruptions occurred. In cases such as these, when the mind perceives something it cannot recognize, it tries to provide an explanation.

A huge headline in the Daily Mirror *proclaims a Loch Ness monster sighting in 1977.*

If it has knowledge of an explanation provided by others, it considers that possibility and makes a suggestion. It may suggest something incredible, which satisfies the ordinary person's yearning for incredible experience. This "auto-suggestion" may lie behind many Loch Ness sightings and the sincere belief of witnesses that the existence of a great beast has been revealed.

The ancient people who faced unknown natural phenomena provided their explanations in the form of spirits, gods, and other forces that acted from their own inexplicable motives. In the twentieth century, there was very little mystery remaining about storms, floods, or volcanoes. The last regions of the completely unknown lie at the mercy of telescopes and laboratories, where experts carry out their research and provide explanations in a language complex and unintelligible to the average person.

Yet many people still yearn for the mysterious. When they ponder all the sightings of the Loch Ness monster, from the Picts and St. Columba down to Mr. and Mrs. Mackay, Tim Dinsdale, and Robert Rines, they credit something incredible and still unknown. They also want to believe there are still myths and monsters. When they travel to the lake, they peer closely at the water, waiting for something to happen that would make them a part of this long mystery. A tree trunk, a diving otter, a standing wave, or a flight of low-lying geese just will not do.

Notes

Chapter One: The Legend

1. Stephen Lyons, "Birth of a Legend," Nova Online, November 2000. www.pbs.org.wgbh/nova/lochness/legend.html.
2. "Life of St. Columba: How an Aquatic Monster Was Driven Off by Virtue of the Blessed Man's Prayer," *Medieval Sourcebook*. www.fordham.edu/halsall/basis/columba-e.html.
3. Steuart Campbell, *The Loch Ness Monster: The Evidence*. Amherst, NY: Prometheus Books, 1997, pp. 13–14.
4. Henry H. Bauer, *The Enigma of Loch Ness: Making Sense of a Mystery*. Urbana: University of Illinois Press, 1988, p. 1.
5. Campbell, *The Loch Ness Monster*, p. 108.
6. Peter Costello, *In Search of Lake Monsters*. London: St. Albans, 1975, p. 29.
7. Quoted in William S. Ellis, "Loch Ness: The Lake and the Legend," *National Geographic*, June 1977, p. 773.
8. Bernard Heuvelmans, *In the Wake of the Sea Serpents*. New York: Hill and Wang, 1968, p. 20.
9. Quoted in "The Spicer Sighting," August 17, 2001. http://ourworld.compuserve.com/homepages/lesj/spicer.htm.

Chapter Two: Early Investigations

10. Bauer, *The Enigma of Loch Ness*, p. 50.
11. Richard Frere, *Loch Ness*. London: J. Murray, 1988, p. 168.
12. Quoted in Campbell, *The Loch Ness Monster*, p. 53.
13. Frere, *Loch Ness*, p. 169.
14. Campbell, *The Loch Ness Monster*, p. 60.

Chapter Three: Healthy Skepticism

15. Quoted in "The House of Lords Report," Dan Taylor's Nessa Project. www.nessaproject.com/lords2.html.
16. Quoted in "One Man, Two Subs, and a Monster," Franklin Pierce Law Center's IP Mall. www.ipmall.fplc.edu/news_activities/RinesNews/rines003.htm.
17. Quoted in Larissa MacFarquhar, "Letter from Scotland: Monster in the Monitor," *New Yorker*, November 27, 2000, p. 142.
18. John P. Wiley, "Cameras, Sonar Close in on Denizen of Loch Ness," *Smithsonian*, June 1976, p. 105.
19. Quoted in Wiley, "Cameras, Sonar Close in on Denizen of Loch Ness," p. 96.
20. Adrian Shine, "Loch Ness 2000 Exhibition: Chronology," The Loch Ness and Morar Project. www.lochnessproject.org.
21. Editors of Time-Life Books, *Mysterious Creatures*. Alexandria, VA: Time-Life Books, 1988, p. 20.

22. Quoted in MacFarquhar, "Letter from Scotland," p. 146.
23. Quoted in "The Beast of Loch Ness," Nova Online. www.pbs.org/wgbh/ nova/lochness.

Chapter Four: Plesiosaur Possibilities

24. Campbell, *The Loch Ness Monster*, p. 14.
25. Frere, *Loch Ness*, p. 174.
26. Ellis, "Loch Ness: The Lake and the Legend," pp. 769, 772.
27. Robert Rines and Sir Peter Scott, "Naming the Loch Ness Monster," *Nature*, December 11, 1975, p. 467.
28. Rines and Scott, "Naming the Loch Ness Monster," pp. 467–68.
29. Campbell, *The Loch Ness Monster*, p. 115.

Chapter Five: Other Explanations

30. W.H. Lehn, "Atmospheric Refraction and Lake Monsters," *Science*, July 13, 1979, p. 185.
31. Lehn, "Atmospheric Refraction and Lake Monsters," p. 183.
32. Shine, "Loch Ness 2000 Exhibition: Chronology."
33. Robert Todd Carroll, "The Skeptic's Dictionary." www.dcn.davis.ca.us/~ btcarrol/skeptic/pareidol.html.
34. "Mystery Unlocked?" *San Francisco Chronicle*, June 27, 2001. www.sfgate.com/c/s.dll/article/cgi?file=/ c/a/2001/06/27/MN109077.dtl.
35. Quoted in Bauer, *The Enigma of Loch Ness*, p. 97.

For Further Reading

Books

Tim Dinsdale, *Loch Ness Monster*, 4th ed. London: Routledge and Kegan Paul, 1982. A compilation of research carried out by the author, a former aerospace engineer who took up the investigation at Loch Ness in the 1960s.

Rupert T. Gould, *The Loch Ness Monster and Others*. New York: University Books, 1969. This reprint of the 1934 London edition is the original book on the Loch Ness monster, written and published at the height of monster mania in the early 1930s.

Amy Owens, *The Complete Visitor's Guide to Loch Ness, Inverness, and the Loch Ness Monster*. London: Mainstream Press, 2001. A handy guidebook for visitors to Loch Ness, detailing the latest events and research on the Loch Ness phenomenon.

Constance Whyte, *More than a Legend*. London: Hamish Hamilton, 1957. A compilation of interviews and eyewitness sightings, which played an important role in the revival of interest in the Loch Ness monster.

Websites

The Legend of Nessie, the Ultimate Loch Ness Monster Site (www.nessie.co.uk). Describes itself as Nessie's "official" website; contains pages on sightings, current research, documented evidence, biographies of researchers, and "Nessie's Diary."

The Loch Ness and Morar Project (www.lochnessproject.org). A very complete archive of scientific research of all kinds at Loch Ness, including biology, zoology, and geology of the region. Also provides a description of current events, the Loch Ness 2000 exhibition, and the Loch Ness and Morar Project, the largest ongoing research into the Loch Ness phenomenon.

Nova Online: The Beast of Loch Ness. (www.pbs.org/wgbh/nova/lochness). Based on the PBS documentary "The Beast of Loch Ness," which is also available on video, this site offers a program transcript and related information on mythical creatures, sonar research, and cryptozoology. The site also includes RealAudio files of eyewitness sightings of the Loch Ness monster.

Scotland Online: Loch Ness Live! (www.lochness.scotland.net/index.cfm). A lighthearted guide to Loch Ness and the monster, including a Loch Ness Web cam, a guide to sightings, postcards, a newsletter, shopping, and a calendar of events and exhibitions.

Works Consulted

Books

Henry H. Bauer, *The Enigma of Loch Ness: Making Sense of a Mystery*. Urbana: University of Illinois Press, 1988. A review of the Loch Ness phenomenon through the eyes of a believer. A twenty-year student of Loch Ness, Bauer very thoroughly documents and evaluates all reported sightings and evidence, but dismisses valid skeptical findings.

Ronald Binns, *The Loch Ness Mystery Solved*. Buffalo, NY: Prometheus Books, 1985. A close, rational look at the evidence for the Loch Ness monster that concludes there is no plausible hard evidence for the existence of an unknown species in the lake.

Steuart Campbell, *The Loch Ness Monster: The Evidence*. Amherst, NY: Prometheus Books, 1997. A thorough examination of the photographic, eyewitness, film, and sonar evidence for the Loch Ness monster, and a skeptical conclusion that the monster does not exist.

Peter Costello, *In Search of Lake Monsters*. London: St. Albans, 1975. A guide through the history of sea serpents and lake monsters, with a long opening section on Loch Ness. Also discusses parallel phenomena in the rest of Europe, North America, and South America.

Editors of Time-Life Books, *Mysterious Creatures*. Alexandria, VA: Time-Life Books, 1988. Illustrated description of fabled beasts through history, from the great sea serpents to the Ogopogo, Sasquatch, Bigfoot, and the Loch Ness monster.

Richard Ellis, *Monsters of the Sea: The Truth About the Loch Ness Monster, the Giant Squid, Sea Serpents, Mermaids, and Other Fantastic Creatures of the Deep*. New York: Lyons Press, 2000. Detailed and very knowledgeable descriptions of all kinds of sea mysteries, from the ancient past to the present.

Richard Frere, *Loch Ness*. London: J. Murray, 1988. An interesting anecdotal description of the geography and history of Loch Ness and the Highlands region, and memories of the author's boyhood while growing up near the lake.

Paul Harrison, *The Encylopedia of the Loch Ness Monster*. London: Robert Hale, 2001. Facts, figures, terms, biographies, and research connected with the Loch Ness monster mystery in the twentieth century.

Bernard Heuvelmans, *In the Wake of the Sea Serpents*. New York: Hill and Wang, 1968. A detailed and expert book on the phenomenon of marine cryptozoology, also known as the study of sea serpents, by a researcher who is widely regarded as the father of cryptozoology. The author presents a long section on the Loch Ness monster. Unfortunately, the book is more than thirty years old and is sorely in need of updating.

Internet Sources

Robert Todd Carroll, "The Skeptic's Dictionary." www.dcn.davis.ca.us/~btcarrol/skeptic/pareidol.html.

"The House of Lords Report," Dan Taylor's Nessa Project. www.nessaproject.com/lords2.html.

"Life of St. Columba: How an Aquatic Monster Was Driven Off by Virtue of the Blessed Man's Prayer," *Medieval Sourcebook*. www.fordham.edu/halsall/basis/columba-e.html.

Stephen Lyons, "Birth of a Legend," Nova Online, November 2000. www.pbs.org.wgbh/nova/lochness/legend.html.

"Mystery Unlocked?" *San Francisco Chronicle*, June 27, 2001. www.sfgate.com/c/s.dll/article/cgi?file=/c/a/2001/06/27/MN109077.dtl.

"One Man, Two Subs, and a Monster," Franklin Pierce Law Center's IP Mall. www.ipmall.fplc.edu/news_activities/RinesNews/rines003.htm.

Adrian Shine, "Loch Ness 2000 Exhibition: Chronology," The Loch Ness and Morar Project. www.lochnessproject.org.

"The Spicer Sighting," August 17, 2001. http://ourworld.compuserve.com/homepages/lesj/spicer.htm.

Periodicals

William S. Ellis, "Loch Ness: The Lake and the Legend," *National Geographic*, June 1977.

W.H. Lehn, "Atmospheric Refraction and Lake Monsters," *Science*, July 13, 1979.

Larissa MacFarquhar, "Letter from Scotland: Monster in the Monitor," *New Yorker*, November 27, 2000.

Robert Rines and Sir Peter Scott, "Naming the Loch Ness Monster," *Nature*, December 11, 1975.

John P. Wiley, "Cameras, Sonar Close in on Denizen of Loch Ness," *Smithsonian*, June 1976.

Index

Picture Credits

Cover Photo: Fortean Picture Library
© AFP/CORBIS, 70
© Bettmann/CORBIS, 19, 21, 22, 30 (both), 43, 57, 59, 72
© Jonathan Blair/CORBIS, 27
Fortean Picture Library, 14, 33, 35, 47, 48, 50, 52 (both), 62, 65, 66, 67, 74, 76, 81, 83
© Hulton/Archive by Getty Images, 9, 13, 29, 37, 39, 44, 61
© Joe McDonald/CORBIS, 71
Brandy Noon, 12, 41
© Leonard de Selva/CORBIS, 17
© Kennan Ward/CORBIS, 77
© Ralph White/CORBIS, 54
© Jim Zuckerman/CORBIS, 56

About the Author

Thomas Streissguth was born in Washington, D.C., and grew up in Minnesota. After earning a B.A. in music, he traveled in Europe and worked as a teacher and book editor. He has written more than thirty books of nonfiction, including histories, biographies, and geographies for children and young adults.